'A clear, practical and powerful look at what it really
r   be the Church today. Sim's experience as a
         ader and his biblical insights create a timely
         e to us all.'
         Anne Calver – Evangelical Alliance, Spring Harvest and
         Baptist Church

'I   of information overload and complexity, this
         much needed. Church "busyness" and church
"   " can often blur the "why". *Simply Church* brings
         to the simple, radical roots of our faith.'
S   ell – Alive Church and Ground Level Network

'S   but not simplistic – this book is a tonic for
a   who senses that the Church is a wonderful
n   but wonders if we've made it too complicated
a   something special. Lots of wisdom here for a
c   vision and a hopeful plan of action!'
P   Harcourt – New Wine England and All Saints Church

'V   e known Sim (and Lottie) since we were
te   ers, and it's a joy to look back at how God has
le   m into leading a church and being an incredible
p   e influence to everyone around them. Sim is
pas   nate about leading church and his passion,
authenticity and love for people is found on every page
of this book.'
Becca and Tim Jupp – Arun Church and Big Church Day Out

'Sim has dedicated his life to building God's Church and has a passion for making church life authentic, active and aligned to its original design and purpose. This is a refreshing read, full of honesty and insight, and shines a light on what really matters in creating a church that ultimately does what it's designed to do.'

Ness Wilson – Pioneer Network and Open Heaven Church

'You can't change the Church unless you love the Church, and Sim is someone who has poured his life into doing just that. One of the things I appreciate about this book is that it's not just theory, but hard-won insight from someone deep in the trenches of local leadership. His practical wisdom shines through every page.'

Pete Greig – Emmaus Rd Church and 24-7 Prayer International

'One of the main reasons for the success of the Early Church as recorded in Acts was its simplicity. It would seem that with every generation since then the Church has become more complicated, and to a large extent lost its *raison d'être* along the way. *Simply Church* can help us find our way back to who we were designed by God to be: His reformatory vehicle. I would recommend this book to anyone who longs to see the dynamic power of God at work through the Church today.'

Agu Irukwu – Jesus House for all Nations, London, and The Redeemed Christian Church of God, UK

Simply Church

It's time for the Church to pause and rethink.
Let's rediscover our relationship with God.

SIM DENDY

First edition published in 2020 by CWR (now Waverley Abbey Resources).
This second edition published in 2021 by Waverley Abbey Resources,
Waverley Abbey House, Waverley Lane, Farnham, Surrey GU9 8EP, UK.
Waverley Abbey Resources is a trading name of CWR. CWR is a Registered
Charity – Number 294387 and a Limited Company registered in England –
Registration Number 1990308.

For a list of National Distributors, visit waverleyabbeyresources.org/distributors
Unless otherwise indicated, Scripture references are taken from the New Living
Translation, Copyright © 1996, 2004, 2007, 2013, 2015 by Tyndale House
Foundation. Used by permission of Tyndale House Publishers Inc., Carol Stream,
Illinois 60188. All rights reserved.

Other versions used: Scripture quotations marked ESV are taken from the
ESV® Bible (The Holy Bible, English Standard Version®). ESV® Text Edition:
2016. Copyright © 2001 by Crossway, a publishing ministry of Good News
Publishers. Scripture quotations marked *The Message* are taken from *THE
MESSAGE*, copyright © 1993, 2002, 2018 by Eugene H. Peterson. Used by
permission of NavPress. All rights reserved. Represented by Tyndale House
Publishers, Inc. Scripture quotations marked NIV are taken from the Holy Bible,
New International Version® Anglicised, NIV® Copyright © 1979, 1984, 2011
by Biblica, Inc.® Used by permission. All rights reserved worldwide. Scripture
quotations marked NKJV are taken from the New King James Version®.
Copyright © 1982 by Thomas Nelson. Used by permission. All rights reserved.
Concept development, editing, design and production by CWR.

Every effort has been made to ensure that this book contains the correct
permissions and references, but if anything has been inadvertently overlooked
the Publisher will be pleased to make the necessary arrangements at the first
opportunity. Please contact the Publisher directly.

Cover design and illustrations: Sam Hubbard
Printed in the UK by Yeomans
ISBN: 978-1-78951-371-4

To the church communities that I have had
the privilege to be a part of.

To those who have prayed for me, invested in me,
believed in me, challenged me, encouraged me,
brought out the best in me and ultimately led me to
a greater love for God and His Church – thank you.

Contents

I love my church

People often talk about what they love. They say they love their spouse, or they love their children. They may say they love their football team, or they love their pets, but how many people say they love their church?

Theologians may point out that it is not 'our' church to love. It is God's Church, which I understand, but I still love my church. I love God's Church. The Church is something I have been privileged to serve for many years and hopefully will continue to do so for many more.

The Church is the hope of the world, and when it works the way it's supposed to, the Church is unbeatable: a community of Jesus-believers who love one another and are committed to sharing a message of hope and transformation with a fragmented world. But I have also seen the Church when things go wrong and people get hurt, frustrated or overlooked. I have experienced all those things personally... and I still love the Church.

I am writing this book, not because I think the Church is broken and I want to point out its faults, but because I believe the Church is the Bride of Christ and I want it to be beautiful and ready.

I have had the privilege of leading many wedding services

and attending many more. I have never seen a bride who was not glowing and full of hope – hopeful of what is to come for her and her husband-to-be, and hopeful for the life ahead.

I am hopeful for the Church. Our world needs the Church, like never before, to be full of hope. But the Church is not always what it could be. It has become complex and complicated. The mystery of Christian faith becomes weird when it is unexplainable.

The Church needs a declutter. A clear-out. A detox.

We all end up collecting excess stuff, whether it be books, clothes, cars, gadgets... thoughts, habits, scars, traditions... or maybe just a few extra pounds. Sometimes, it's good to strip things back a bit. It's healthy to occasionally explore our past and consider a fresh purpose for the future.

To turn the computer off, wait for a moment and then reboot.

To realign ourselves with the plan that our creator God has already set out for us.

To recalibrate.

To return to the start again.

To go back a couple of millennia to discover what the original Church looked like, so we can remember and reset.

Simply... Church.

I'd like to run with the idea that discontentment is actually a gift to the Church. If you are someone who has the ability to see the things that are wrong in the Church and in the world, then thank God for that insight and discernment. Not everyone has the eyes to see, or to notice, or to care. I want us to see that discontentment is not a reason to *disengage* from the Church but a reason to *engage* with it.

Jesus offered an alternative to Caesar's empire not by
mounting a rebellion but by teaching people that another

way is possible. That way is wonderfully summarised in Jesus' triumphal entry, the inaugural parade of a new kind of king for a new kind of kingdom. Church history is filled with holy dissenters, rabble-rousers and prophets — disturbers of the peace who've helped to show us a better way. As some historians have pointed out, every few hundred years the church gets cluttered up and infected with the materialism and militarism of the world around it. We begin to forget who we are. One bishop said, 'And so every five hundred years or so the church needs a rummage sale' – to get rid of the clutter and remember the true treasures of our faith.[1]

My prayer is that as you read this book, you may discover (or re-discover) the purpose of the Church, that we might help shape our churches of today into healthy communities that better reflect the incredible God we serve.

Why Church?

Start with the why

When studying for my master's degree in theology and leadership, I chose to do my dissertation on the role of the local church. As part of my research, I recorded interviews with five very experienced church leaders, with a minimum of 20 years' leadership experience, and each from a different type of church. They were an Anglican vicar, a Baptist minister, an Assemblies of God pastor, a New Church leader and an Elim pastor – you get the picture, a variety of leaders. I sent each participant the set of questions that I intended to use for the interview so they could prepare their answers. I included a few warm-up questions (Who are you? How did you get into church leadership?), mainly as a way of putting them at ease before the 'real' interview began.

But what intrigued me most was the answers I got to one of my supposed 'warm-up' questions: 'What do you understand to be the purpose of the local church?'

I thought it would be really simple. I thought these experienced leaders, who had led churches for 20+ years, would be really sure what they were trying to lead people into. But, after they had been given time to think about it, the answers they gave me were surprisingly lengthy, cautious and muddled. These experienced church leaders described the purpose of the local church using phrases such as, 'proclaiming the kingdom of God in a prophetic kingdom way' – and I still don't know what that means. Don't get me wrong: these are friends of mine, good people who love Jesus and serve Him and their communities faithfully, yet still they struggled to verbalise the purpose of the local church.

Surely it should be easier to explain? Surely the Church should be simple to understand for the non-believer and the believer?

Maybe I am the problem. I've been criticised for being too simplistic in the way that I lead, the 'depth' of my preaching or my seemingly naive approach to life. But I believe that if the Church is not easy to understand and access, then people will ignore it and choose to spend time doing something that they do understand, and give their energy and passion to that instead.

I was brought up in a Christian home and my dad was a local church pastor (the last thing I ever wanted to become!). As a family with six children we would regularly attend church, and one by one each of us made a clear decision to follow Jesus for ourselves and give our lives to Him.

When it was my turn, I told my mum that I wanted to give my life to Jesus on a day I would remember, so, with my fourth birthday coming up, I suggested that that would be a great day to say yes to following Jesus. Of course, on the day itself I was far too excited by the presents, the party and the cake to remember my eternal destiny. So that night as my mum tucked me into bed, with the sugar rush finally starting to wear off, she quietly reminded me of my idea to use my birthday as the day I would give my life to Christ. It felt like a perfect end to a perfect day (birthdays are always better when you are a child, aren't they?). I made that decision on 1 February 1978. See, my theory worked – I will never forget that date.

Over the next few years I repeated that simple prayer at various church events, summer camps and youth weekends away. I knew I was saved, but as I got older my understanding of my faith and the church I was part of all seemed to get more complicated. Life was looming ahead of me; I had lots of decisions to make that would affect my future, and where I fitted into church seemed more complex than when I was small (my dad was the pastor – I went because I had to!). When I was a child, everything seemed so easy. Why and when did it get complicated?

As a grown-up, I have discovered that sometimes people like to make church matters complicated, either because they don't quite understand it, or they don't want others to participate and so keep the mystery of God's family to themselves. But in my Bible (and hopefully yours as well), Jesus said:

> 'Let the little children come to me, and do not hinder them, for the kingdom of heaven belongs to such as these.'
> Matthew 19:14 (NIV)

I believe church should be simple. Easy to understand. For those who are like these children.

But simple things are not always easy.

> *Simplicity is complex. It's never simple to keep things simple. Simple solutions require the most advanced thinking.*[2]

I don't know about 'advanced thinking', but it's my aim to distil down some of our seemingly over-complicated ideas, see what we can learn from the Early Church, and create some simpler concepts to help us understand the Church better (so that we can dress her as a beautiful Bride, not an ugly stepsister).

So, let's start with the 'why'.

Why did you start going to church? Was it because, like me, your family went so you just found yourself joining in? Or did a friend invite you? Was there a good-looking girl or guy attending the church so you thought it might improve your chances if you went along? Were you going through a time of challenge and crisis and needed some help? Did you come to faith through an Alpha course or Christianity Explored, and feel at home at the church that hosted it? Were you lonely and looking for a place of belonging? Did you watch a church run great community projects, such as working with the homeless, those in debt or a food bank, and start volunteering – to then be drawn into the church itself?

In 2010, Simon Sinek gave a TED Talk called 'Start With Why'.[3] It was one of the first to go viral, and has been watched by millions. Right at the centre of his talk (and corresponding book) is his clear concept of the 'why' and its importance to people and organisations. He draws what he calls the 'golden circle', which looks like an archery target made up of three circles. Sinek suggests that the outside ring is WHAT an organisation does, the middle ring is HOW the organisation does what it does and the inner ring is WHY they do it.

He suggests that every organisation knows WHAT they do (garages repair cars; supermarkets sell food; schools educate students). Most are clear on HOW they do it (the values they hold; their style and approach; their unique selling point). But according to Sinek, very few organisations know WHY they do what they do.

He suggests that while people are interested in knowing WHAT you do, they are infinitely more inspired when they discover WHY you do it.

This is also true of the Church. We often know WHAT we do (Sunday services, youth groups, social transformation etc), and we often know HOW to do it (after all, we have been providing some

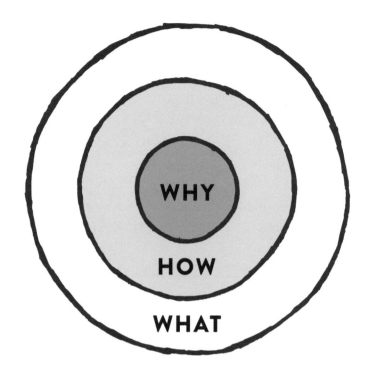

of our services for centuries), but the Church is often unable to articulate WHY we do it.

How many times have you sat through church notices when, in talking about a future activity, they will promote the time and place of the event, but nothing about *why* people should go?

When we fully understand our WHY, it makes such a difference to the HOW and the WHAT. When we understand the purpose behind our existence, it helps everything else make sense. To discover our God-given WHY, we need to go backwards so we can go forwards.

Ten hallmarks

Like any organisation, the Church can drift and become complex. If we forget why it was started in the first place – if we lose the passion of the pioneers – what can happen is we end up becoming 'managers', maintaining the systems, routines and policies, but having forgotten *why*.

Sometimes, a detox is required. It's a bit like the January that follows a well-enjoyed (but perhaps slightly over-indulged) Christmas, when we are willing to adopt a significant change of lifestyle to clean out our systems and get back to normal. If it works for our physical bodies, does it work for the Body of Christ? If our churches are a little out of shape, having gone a little overboard on the politics, coffee rotas, debates over flag-waving and discussions over sound levels, perhaps we need a church detox to get us back in shape and ready for action.

So what does a healthy church look like? What are the hallmarks of a healthy church community?

If we want to be authentic, we need to imitate the original – not a replica. Let's say an apprentice builder was tasked to cut a large number of planks of wood to a specific size. He decided that rather than measuring each piece of wood using a tape measure, he would simply use the last length he cut to measure the next length, and so on. After cutting a number of planks, however, he realised that no two planks were the same length. The tape measure was the original source, but he had used replicas to measure against instead.

In the same way, there are many great 'replica' churches throughout the world with some excellent ideas; there are some amazing church planting conferences, podcasts, books, blogs and websites full of helpful information. And while it is important that we learn from each other, let's also ensure that we stay on track with biblical guidelines of what a church community should look like by regularly checking the tape measure and going back to the original: the very first church from the book of Acts.

The writer of Acts was the Gospel writer Luke, a doctor and author who had been commissioned by the wealthy Theophilus to carefully study the life of Jesus and His followers, and record his findings. Today these are the Gospel of Luke, which he thoughtfully named after himself, and the book of Acts (sometimes also known as the Acts of the Apostles).

The Gospel of Luke is the narrative of Jesus through His birth, life, ministry, death and resurrection in great detail. In Acts, Luke starts with Jesus instructing His disciples in sharing the message of the gospel throughout the world before He ascends back to heaven. This is a significant moment for the disciples. Jesus has completed His 33 years on earth, and His mission is now complete. His three-year national preaching tour had been a sell-out and His internship programme was a huge success. Now, His followers left behind are trying to work out what they do with this new understanding of Jesus being the Messiah. How do they follow Him when He is not physically there to ask practical questions about how to feed thousands of people, or to wake up next time the sea gets a little choppy?

Confused and uncertain about what to do next, they gather to vote on who gets the role of treasurer (since Judas Iscariot vacated the role), and then they pray. And what a prayer meeting! The Holy Spirit, promised by Jesus, appears with great power: tongues of fire spread throughout the room, they speak in new languages and thousands get saved in response to Peter's first ever preach (if only all of our prayer meetings could be like that). Then what?

They have thousands of people wanting to join the disciples in following this person called Jesus, who is no longer with them. They start to gather regularly to share stories and worship God, thanking Him for sending His Son Jesus – and then this new movement, initially known as 'The Way', starts to emerge. Little do any of them realise that this is the birth of the first ever church and that every year at Pentecost, for centuries to come, billions of Christians around the world will remember this moment and thank God for Peter and the Early Church fathers.

So, what did the Early Church look like? In Acts 2:42–47 we have a great description of this new community that provides ten hallmarks of an authentic church:

> All the believers devoted themselves to the apostles' teaching, and to fellowship, and to sharing in meals (including the Lord's Supper), and to prayer. A deep sense of awe came over them all, and the apostles performed many miraculous signs and wonders. And all the believers met together in one place and shared everything they had. They sold their property and possessions and shared the money with those in need. They worshiped together at the Temple each day, met in homes for the Lord's Supper, and shared their meals with great joy and generosity — all the while praising God and enjoying the goodwill of all the people. And each day the Lord added to their fellowship those who were being saved.
>
> Acts 2:42–47

As we go through this passage, we can see ten 'hallmarks' that are essential to any authentic church.

1. Preaching up a storm

The early Christians were devoted to listening to the apostles as they brought the words of Jesus to life, revealing the mysteries of ancient scriptures (v42). There was a hunger for learning from those who were recently saved. There is the same hunger today. We must not stop preaching from the Bible. I have heard it said that in a fast-moving world, people don't want to sit for half an hour to listen to someone read from an ancient text. So there may be a challenge to the preachers out there to find creative ways to bring the message to life, but let's *never* stop preaching and teaching. There are more resources out there than ever before to help communicators unpack the Bible and find a way that works, but whatever we do, we need to keep the Bible at the heart of the Church. It brings life. It contains the very power of God Himself – accounts of what God has done and what He will do. Our teaching of the Bible needs to be done in a way that is bold, radical, relevant, theologically sound, Christ-centred, thought-provoking and transformational. (No pressure...)

2. Fellowship

It's God's Church, which He is responsible for building, but it is also a partnership between God the Holy Spirit and us as His people. The earth was created out of community within the Trinity: God wants to be in community with us, and He loves it when we are in relationship with each other. That is how He designed us. God chooses to use us in His mission, in a dynamic partnership that changes the world daily. Jesus Himself challenged His disciples on how they related to each other and stopped them from vying for the top spot. Our biggest challenge as the Church is not the world 'out there' – it is often the way we treat each other. As Dave Smith says, we need to do the root work before the fruit work.[4] If we want to be successful as a church community, we need to work hard at our relationships with each other and find various ways to gather together to celebrate the God that joins us as one.

3. Food!

Meals are such an important part of building community. I love the fact that Luke mentions that when the believers shared meals together (not forgetting Communion), which they did regularly, they did so *with joy*. I wonder how many Christians invite people into their homes out of a sense of duty rather than joy. The art of the 'slow meal' has often been lost in our Western culture. We see food and eating as a necessity, rather than an important ritual of connecting and re-connecting with family and friends. It's important that we take time to eat with people, to find out who they really are and what they are passionate about, all while we relax and enjoy some delicious food. We need to build a community of friendships, not just useful contacts.

4. Prayer

The early believers 'devoted themselves... to prayer' (v42). It's so important we do the same. Why? Prayer is where we build a deeper relationship with our Father God. Prayer is where we truly win; winning the battle over our circumstances, our relationships, our work challenges and our family's needs all comes through prayer and fasting. In the same way that Jesus regularly prayed and received power from His Father God, so it is the same for us. Prayer unites us. Prayer connects us. I am convinced that the Church will never grow through structures and systems alone, but through prayer – deliberate, intentional, consistent prayer: Your kingdom come; Your will be done. It changes our churches and more importantly it changes us. It will never be through our clever efforts alone, but by God changing the spiritual atmosphere.

5. Awe, signs and wonders

When did you last sense awe in your church? Was it the time someone thought it would be a good idea to use a live donkey for the Christmas service just after you'd installed the new carpet? We need to regain the awe that comes from walking in step with the Holy Spirit. Miraculous signs and wonders are not just words, they are a real, active part of a vibrant church today. I know some of this beautiful awe has been damaged by churches chasing the gifts and not the giver, but don't stop pursuing God and being brave to ask Him for more. See what happens. Keep asking, keep waiting as He promises to send His Holy Spirit to be your comforter and provider. Yes, I believe our Sunday meetings should be accessible to all, but let's still be open to the work of the Holy Spirit. It might be messy, but that's OK. It's neat and tidy in the graveyard where there is no life. It's messy in the nursery, but that's where new life is.

6. Better together

A few years ago, the concept of 'deconstruction' of churches emerged – the idea that the Church didn't need to meet regularly as we should be involved in our communities, and that wherever we were as followers of Christ, 'we were the Church'. I understand the thinking, but it totally overlooks the importance of meeting together. We are better when we are together, but our gathering in itself is not the ultimate purpose: our gatherings are to prepare us for the mission of being sent into all the world. Without meeting together, there is limited preparation of the saints. The Church becomes invisible without a clearly defined community that each member can belong to, knowing they are needed and known.

7. Share the wealth

I find it fascinating that every household on my street has a lawnmower, but it's rare that we all mow our lawns at the same time. In theory, it would only require *one* lawnmower to meet the needs of the whole street... yet we would all rather have our own one and never lend it to anyone. We live in a world of excess stuff where the idea of sharing our belongings brings many of us out in a rash – even if it's the camping equipment stored in the loft, which we haven't used for a decade.

Sharing requires vulnerability, and an element of risk. Someone who is in need also needs to be brave enough to let others know that they need help. This enables those with resources the ability to offer support, not knowing if their offer will be accepted or acceptable. But these mutually beneficial interactions create deeper levels of relationship and build stronger communities. The problem is, someone needs to go first. Someone has to be brave and take the risk of loaning that under-utilised tool from your shed, never knowing if it will be returned at all, let alone in the same condition. But what do you really have to lose?

8. Live generously

Sharing the lawnmower is one thing, but giving money in a way that affects our wallet is counter-cultural on a different level. We see finances as a transactional tool. We believe that we have earned our income for the work that we have done – why should we then give it away to someone who, in our opinion, has done nothing to warrant it? 'It's *my* money. I've worked hard for it.' Our bank statements are, in a way, our spiritual documentation of what's most important to each of us. If we love fashion, food, family, cars, homes, technology or holidays, then it will be reflected in what we spend our money on. Money is powerful. How we relate to it, rely on it and release it says a lot about our attitudes and our hearts.

9. Worship

First and foremost, we are called to be worshippers of the awe-inspiring, star-flinging, mountain-making creator God. It is His Church and always will be. If God and our worship of Him is not the focus of the church that we are part of, then its attention has become diverted from its original purpose. The reason the Early Church gathered in the first place is that each individual had had an encounter with the Son of God, and for many this would have been firsthand. They had individually experienced His love for them personally. Why wouldn't they want to worship and praise Him for His love, grace and gift of salvation? And even though 2,000 years have gone by since the Church began, we can still encounter Jesus who is alive today. It is this encounter that draws us to others who have had a similar experience. Whether we worship with a pipe organ, guitars, drums, DJ decks or a full orchestra, let's create an environment in which we truly 'Let everything that has breath praise the LORD' (Psa. 150:6, NIV).

10. Home is where the heart is

They say the Englishman's home is his castle. Our safe space; our shelter; our statement of achievement; the place where we can be fully ourselves, where no one else can see us. To invite a bunch of people from church into that space is, for many of us, a step too far. Surely the biblical concept of 'meeting in homes' was a cultural one only? We now have places for community: church buildings, pubs, cinemas, parks, coffee shops and restaurants. Surely, we don't need people to come into our *homes*, right?

Our Sunday services might be incredible times of worship and encounter, and our local independent coffee shop a beautiful place to enjoy a cappuccino, but our homes are where we are really known. We can connect on a much deeper level in a more intimate setting. It's great to gather in crowds, but people want to be known as a person and not just a number. As we open our homes to others and offer simple hospitality, we move from building connections to creating genuine friendships.

Based on these hallmarks, then, a fully detoxed, simply defined, authentic church, based on the original model, should be a community of people who:

- Love the Bible and teach it well
- Make the most of opportunities to spend time with each other
- Enjoy sharing Communion and eating together with a sense of fun
- Understand the power of prayer and can't help but do it all the time
- Work in partnership with the Holy Spirit as an everyday activity
- Look for ways to get together in a large crowd to celebrate
- Hold things lightly and share what they have
- Give generously, not afraid to buy the first round of drinks
- Love worshipping and praising their creator God
- Open their homes up to each other, always having room for one more

As the Early Church hung out together, worshipped God and loved each other with all that they had, the Bible says that they '[enjoyed] the goodwill of all the people. And each day the Lord added to their number' (Acts 2:47, NIV). These hallmarks are helpful, but we still need to clarify the vision for our churches – in other words, *why do we do church?*

Soon after I joined Freedom Church as the Senior Leader, I got to work on our vision and mission statement. Having read lots of books on leadership, and having been to endless conferences on church and leadership specifically, I thought I knew what I was doing. When I finally came up with what I thought was the perfect vision statement, I did what so many husbands do: mention it to my wife while driving (I'm not sure why we do it when we are driving… maybe we feel safer?). I recited this amazing vision statement to my wife, Lottie, while she politely listened, and then paused (never a good sign!). Her feedback: 'It sounds more like a political party broadcast – and doesn't even mention Jesus.'

Now, I know no one particularly loves getting criticism, but my response to this was automatically defensive.

'What do you mean, it doesn't mention Jesus? It doesn't have to! Everyone will know we are all about Jesus – we are a church!' But despite my protestation, I had the sinking feeling that once again my wife was right and I needed to listen.

Lottie was bang on the money, seeing right through my effort to create a system of church while forgetting the very reason why it might exist in the first place. I had created an unhealthy concept, making the assumption that everyone would somehow know what was right at the heart of why we do what we do as a church, without making it clear and simple.

I knew I needed to get back on my knees and rewrite our vision.

Eventually, after much prayer and conversation, we came up with a vision of the Freedom Church we longed to see in our future. We then created a clear mission process that established four elements, which we initially referred to as our 'Contagious DNA' (a grand way of saying 'values' – but why say 'values' when you can say 'Contagious DNA'?!). We wrapped these values around the core of our vision: to lead people in the pursuit of Jesus to see lives and communities transformed. That's it. Simple.

Great concepts always sound simple to the one with the original idea. John F. Kennedy probably thought it was a simple enough idea to put a man on the moon; simple can often drift towards complex.

I love the local church, and we need to find ways to keep it from getting complex.

Sounds simple, but might not be as easy as it sounds...

Mission drift

It's all well and good establishing a vision statement or outlining a mission process; the challenge is staying on task. The most important question any leader should be asking is, 'Are we still on track to achieve the vision?' If not, you need to make some changes – fast. When sailing on the ocean, the smallest degree of deviation off-course could lead you to miss your destination by hundreds of miles.

As the Church, we need to stay sharp and 'on mission'. We need to keep reminding ourselves of WHY we do WHAT we do, and that we are fully consumed by Jesus and what He has done for us, rather than simply being consumers of the church programme and 'what the church can do for me'.

After the Challenger Space Shuttle disaster of 1986, NASA came up with the phrase 'normalisation of deviation', where departure from the original mission, for all kinds of reasons, becomes the norm. In retail, if no one is buying your product, you know that you have to change something quickly or you will soon go bust. But when a business experiences normalisation of deviation, it often ends badly. Remember Blockbuster Video? In 1991 it was the world leader in video rental, worth around $8.4 billion. But by 2010 it was losing over $1 billion a year as no one wanted to rent DVDs (let alone video cassettes!) anymore. A business that had been on every high street soon disappeared. Then there's Kodak, who'd been specialist photo developers for over a century before collapsing, having failed to adapt their business model in a world where photography no longer required film. A number of gigantic and famous businesses, wildly successful in their prime, have since vanished because they took their eye off the ball.

It's not just big businesses that can be affected by normalisation of deviation. Every day people are delegated simple tasks, but somehow manage to end up forgetting to complete the one task they had to achieve. It happens to me most days. My wife asks me to put the bin out on my way to work, and I say, 'Sure, no problem!' Then I walk out the door, wonder where I've put my car keys and why the kids have left their bikes on the drive... and before I know it, I've driven off without putting the bin out. It's not deliberate, but subtle distractions can take us off task.

It's amazing how easily we can get stuck into our 'bit' of church and complain about the things that don't suit us – elements that are not how we would prefer to do them. It's easy to miss the point and allow the mission to drive past us, while we're distracted by our intense focus on the small element of church that we have decided is the most important.

The thing is, the great commission hasn't changed. It still requires us to pursue the call of Jesus:

> Jesus came and told his disciples, 'I have been given all authority in heaven and on earth. Therefore, go and make disciples of all the nations, baptizing them in the name of the Father and the Son and the Holy Spirit. Teach these new disciples to obey all the commands I have given you. And be sure of this: I am with you always, even to the end of the age.'
> Matthew 28:18–20

Staying sharp and keeping it simple all sounds good, but doesn't fully give us a WHY. Sure, understanding the Early Church and how they operated is useful around the WHAT we should be doing, and reminding ourselves of the great commission is timely. But WHY do we do church? Why do we sing songs? Why do we run social justice projects? Why do we run small groups in our homes? Why run Alpha courses? WHY?

Why do we do church today?

Theologian and Catholic priest Raniero Cantalamessa said the following:

> The love of God is the answer to all the whys in the Bible, the why of creation, the why of incarnation, the why of redemption... If the written word of the Bible could be changed into a spoken word and become one single voice, this voice, more powerful than the roaring sea would cry out 'The Father Loves You'.[5]

God's love is the why.

God's love is so great that He sent His only Son Jesus to die on a cross for us – to take our place – to receive a punishment that He didn't deserve.

> For this is how God loved the world: He gave his one and only Son, so that everyone who believes in him will not perish but have eternal life.
> John 3:16

God's love kept Jesus on the cross.

We do church because we want to express God's love to a hurting world. We run community projects because of God's love. We write songs and books because of God's love. It's why we do what we do.

We live in a broken world, surrounded by people struggling with finances, work, relationships, education, addiction – and we have the answer to the world's needs. There are thousands of people within our reach who don't know that Jesus loves them when they feel unloved, or that He has a plan and purpose for them when they feel lost.

So if God's love is so great that He sent His Son to die for us, then it's only right that we stay focused on keeping the main thing the main thing, and not allowing mission drift to happen. God's love is what started this adventure of faith, and it's His love that keeps us pursuing the purpose that He has set before us. It's all about Jesus' love for us, and how we show that love to others. It's living life how Jesus did: with love.

To avoid drifting, we need to keep on reminding ourselves why we do what we do. We can get sucked into church business, but it was never about the organisation. It was for normal, everyday people that Christ died.

The Church is the storyteller of hope.

God's love is why we keep telling the story.

Come, follow me

We've already looked at ten hallmarks of a healthy church culture, but the Church does not exist just to have a healthy culture. It has a mission. A purpose. A reason for existing.

When Jesus started His season of ministry, He invited His first disciples to join Him on the adventure of a lifetime when He said to them:

> 'Come, follow me, and I will show you how to fish for people!'
> Matthew 4:19

These are significant words from Jesus, which hold four foundational principles to the very purpose and mission of the Church. We can break this famous phrase into four sections:

1. Come
2. Follow me
3. I will show you how to
4. Fish for people

Essentially, this is what Jesus was saying to His freshly picked disciples:

- *Come.* 'You are welcome; everyone is invited; there is access for all; I want my house to be full.'
- *Follow me.* 'I have something to share with you; I am the great teacher; I am going somewhere; walk with me.'
- *I will show you how to.* 'I will set the example; I won't just talk about it; I will demonstrate so that you can have a go yourself.'
- *Fish for people.* 'It's not just about you. I have a bigger mission that is for others that will reach across the world.'

I'd like to submit that these four principles, that formed part of the invitation to the original twelve disciples, offer us a guide as to how we can structure our churches today to ensure they are as authentic as possible. (Throughout the rest of the book we will use these four principles to guide us as we unpack the ten hallmarks.) Considering each of these four principles as a 'quadrant', I believe that if one of them is missing, it will limit the potential of that church to fulfil the mission that Jesus invited His disciples – and us – to participate in.

'Come'	**ENCOUNTER**	because everyone can experience God
'Follow me'	**GATHER**	because together is always better
'I will show you how to'	**GROW**	because no one is finished yet
'Fish for people'	**INFLUENCE**	because every person can create change

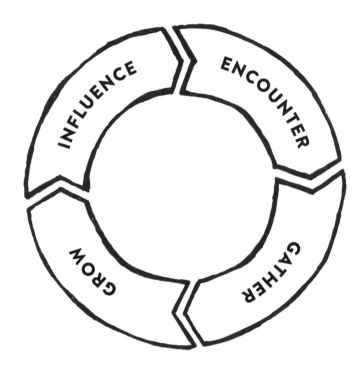

I know I am in danger of oversimplifying, but simplicity brings clarity – and I would rather have a church that is clear in its purpose than a church so complex that no one knows what they should do next.

I believe these four things are central to shaping the mission of the local church. Although there is never an exact formula for anyone's journey to faith, these four processes are also representative of a new believer's path to finding Jesus and growing as a disciple. It often starts with an ENCOUNTER with God through an event or meeting one of His people, followed by an invitation to GATHER in some kind of church setting (whether it be a Sunday service or a group that meets in a home). Then they GROW in their faith with others and learn to INFLUENCE the world around them, so that they too can one day help someone ENCOUNTER God for themselves. And so, it goes on. It's actually a cyclical process that you can join at any point, and then invite others to participate with you.

Let me give you an example. Paul is a special member of our church. When we launched the idea of running a local food bank in our community, he turned up to the very first volunteers evening. I remember meeting him as he nervously paced outside the room, building up the courage to come in and meet people. Paul struggled with anxiety and large crowds but wanted to get involved. He had benefitted from the food bank in the past and now wanted the opportunity to help others. Paul became a special volunteer that everyone soon knew very well. We discovered that once he became comfortable with the group, he would love to chat... for ages. As we got to know Paul, one of our team invited him to the Alpha course, which he came to each week – and then made the decision to follow Jesus. He joined a 'connect group' in our church to start off with, while he built up the courage to come to our larger gathering on a Sunday. With the encouragement of his connect group, he started coming on Sundays, and then decided to get baptised – an absolutely glorious moment in the sunshine outside on our annual church weekend away. Now he regularly meets with his group to learn and grow, and has started to invite others to come along as well. He has even appeared on TV for our local BBC network promoting the work of Christians Against Poverty. I remember proudly standing in the room, watching him being interviewed by the local reporter as he told his story of coming to faith so clearly.

Paul had *encountered* God for himself, started to *gather* with others regularly, is *growing* in his faith and is now having great *influence* on others.

I want Paul's story to be replicated in all of our churches many times over.

Encounter

Everyone can
experience God

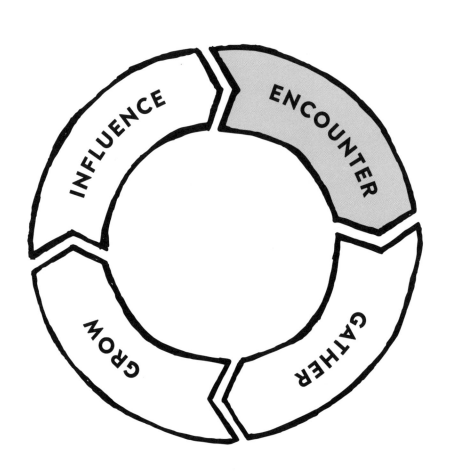

Encounter is for all

> Therefore welcome one another as Christ has welcomed you, for the glory of God.
>
> Romans 15:7 (ESV)

Can everyone really encounter God? Is it even possible, or just a nice catchphrase that makes us feel more inclusive as a church? Jesus simply said 'Come' to those He invited to follow Him, but sometimes, perhaps through our language, style, cliques or expectations, we can end up making our churches some pretty unwelcoming communities that do not truly represent Jesus and the heart He has for people.

Most people's first encounter with God comes after encountering one of His people. How we present ourselves as Christians, and as a church, will either point people towards our heavenly Father or divert them away from Him. Everything we do or say communicates something – from the first face-to-face welcome to the way we speak about people when they are not in the room, and the way we behave when we think we are not being watched. As Christians, we represent God on earth and regularly have the opportunity to reveal God's majesty and wonder to those around us.

So what does a church that is really accessible to everyone actually look like? What might be attractive to one group of people will be off-putting to others. At Freedom Church we often use the phrase 'everyone's welcome', but is that even possible?

Making people feel welcome is a real talent and, to speak plainly, not everyone has it. When visiting churches in the past, I have often been amazed that the volunteer placed on the door is, ironically, the last person who really wants to be there. There is no eye contact, no smile of welcome – just a mumbled 'hello' that is barely audible and an uncomfortable look that says, 'I would rather be quite literally anywhere else.' I don't say this to be critical, but to point out that people make their first impressions very quickly. Let's get our most welcoming people on our welcoming teams, and find another job for those who aren't naturally 'people' people (they will be relieved, and so will your new guests).

If we assume that creating a 'church for all' requires us to become lukewarm and bland, we end up standing for nothing; we become an irrelevance. People are not attracted to 'safe and boring' – people want an adventure! They want to be part of something with a purpose, where they can be a team member on the journey, and feel needed and known.

The concept of welcome is really important. It's a value that I hold to dearly, because I have been in churches where people have been made to feel so very unwelcome. Perhaps the smartly dressed elderly person looks the teenager up and down and makes it very clear that they are not suitably attired to meet the almighty God in 'their' church this morning. Or the middle-class parent whispers to their children not to play with children from the 'other' part of town. Maybe there's a team member providing refreshments while making it very clear to the person they are serving that having more than one sugar in their cup of tea is, in their mind, excessive.

Everyone is welcome in the house of God. That will always be my starting point. I find it incredibly offensive that anyone who would profess to love Jesus, and want to imitate Him by the way they live their lives, would even consider rejecting someone made in the image of their creator (Matthew 25 reminds us that one day we will be accountable for the way we treat strangers in their time of need). But there is also the challenge that if we try to be attractive to all, we will be attractive to no one.

It's important to get some clarity on what is unique to each church. Maybe it is the worship music, the children's programme, the work in the community or the age demographic that is served. Find the space and fill it. There are plenty of other churches around, so if people don't feel that one church is the right fit, then we can help them find the space that does work. And even if someone doesn't 'fit', we can still give them a great welcome and make them feel valued. Some of our church members don't love our worship style, but they love the church community (or the coffee we serve!) – so they stay. People don't stay because of our efficient systems; they stay because of the people they meet in our churches, and how they make them feel.

All-inclusive

I really believe that the task of creating a culture of welcome needs to be shared across all generations, from the youngest to the oldest. We need to teach our children to be part of a welcoming community; to look out for others and help them feel at home. If we wait until our kids have become adults before we get them involved, we will look around and they won't be there anymore. Part of the welcoming skill is to train new people to welcome others in. You know someone is feeling at home in your house, for example, when they start opening the door for others, offering them a drink and showing them to their seat without anyone asking them to do so. That reveals something of the culture that has been created.

It might not make us very comfortable to admit it, but let's face it: historically, the Church has not been great at being inclusive. While being interviewed at Greenbelt Festival, Archbishop of Canterbury Justin Welby said he is 'constantly consumed with horror'[6] at the way the Church has handled certain issues. If we're honest, when we consider how Jesus operated, we have so often got it wrong. One of His most famous illustrations is the parable of the prodigal son:

> A man had two sons. The younger son told his father, 'I want my share of your estate now before you die.' So his father agreed to divide his wealth between his sons.
> A few days later this younger son packed all his belongings and moved to a distant land, and there he wasted all his money in wild living. About the time his money ran out, a great famine swept over the land, and he began to starve. He persuaded a local farmer to hire him, and the man sent him into his fields to feed the pigs. The young man became so hungry that even the pods he was feeding the pigs looked good to him. But no one gave him anything.
> When he finally came to his senses, he said to himself, 'At home even the hired servants have food enough to spare, and here I am dying of hunger! I will go home to my father and say, "Father, I have sinned against both heaven and you, and I am no longer worthy of being called your son. Please take me on as a hired servant."'
> So he returned home to his father. And while he was still a long way off, his father saw him coming. Filled with love and

> compassion, he ran to his son, embraced him, and kissed
> him. His son said to him, 'Father, I have sinned against
> both heaven and you, and I am no longer worthy of being
> called your son.'
> But his father said to the servants, 'Quick! Bring the finest
> robe in the house and put it on him. Get a ring for his finger
> and sandals for his feet. And kill the calf we have been
> fattening. We must celebrate with a feast, for this son of
> mine was dead and has now returned to life. He was lost,
> but now he is found.' So the party began.
> Luke 15:11–24

And to add another extraordinary layer of inclusivity to Jesus' example, He told this parable while sitting and eating with the despised and marginalised:

> Tax collectors and other notorious sinners often came to
> listen to Jesus teach. This made the Pharisees and teachers
> of religious law complain that he was associating with such
> sinful people—even eating with them!
> Luke 15:1–2

When surrounded by 'notorious sinners', Jesus' response was to pull up a chair, enjoy a simple meal and share the love of God with them – probably knowing it would annoy the religious leaders looking on.

This is the point: whatever you've done, whatever your story, whatever your past, whatever your disappointments... everyone's welcome.

The house rules

Recently, my wife and I celebrated our wedding anniversary, and Lottie was keen to go on a spa weekend away. I had never been to a spa but, keen to please, I found us a beautiful hotel in mid-Sussex with spa facilities (and some intriguing-sounding beauty treatments). The problem was, I didn't know the rules. I had never been to a place like this and didn't how to behave. They handed me a towel and bathrobe with little in the way of instruction, and I really wasn't sure what I was meant to do, where to get changed or what I should do once I got changed. I initially felt very uncomfortable (although, to be honest, once I knew what I was doing, I quite enjoyed lounging around in a white bathrobe, doing absolutely nothing for a whole day!).

It's often a bit uncomfortable when we go somewhere for the first time. The first day you take your child to school. The first time you eat at an expensive restaurant. That first time you visit the home of your new girlfriend or boyfriend, and all their family stare at you as they try to work out whether or not you are a 'keeper'.

This is what it can feel like for people who are attending church for the first time: where should I sit? Who do I talk to? Where are the toilets? Can I work out the quickest escape route? When do I stand? Do I sing the songs or quietly hum? Do I put my hands up during the singing? Do I put money in the offering bowl based on the quality of the music or as a tip for the preacher? Though you're probably perfectly used to how things work by now, it's worth considering how newcomers might experience your church – while most people are confidently striding around in their bathrobes, so to speak, who might be nervously hanging back in the changing rooms?

This is what it can feel like for people new to church, which is why we try to help people feel at home. You may have heard this sort of thing illustrated before with the three Bs: behave, believe, belong. If people don't feel welcome in our churches, perhaps it's because they're under the impression that if they *behave* the way they should, and *believe* exactly what we do, then, and only then, will they *belong* in our churches. But it should always be the other way round. First of all, they absolutely belong. From that sense of belonging, they believe in what the church is doing and why it exists. Then, quite naturally, they behave like followers of Jesus, in response to His amazing love. A person's beliefs and behaviour is largely down to them. Their sense of belonging in church is largely down to... the church.

The fact is, everyone is welcome because that's what has been modelled to each of us by God Himself.

Worth the risk

The challenge is: what does it really look like to welcome *everyone*? What if it might upset the applecart? Newcomers might disturb the status quo and mess up the comfortable club that our church might have become.

But welcoming all people is *always* worth the risk. Didn't God actively pursue us?

> God showed his great love for us by sending Christ to die for
> us while we were still sinners.
> Romans 5:8

God took the risk with us, so how can we not take the risk with others?

Tim, one of our church leaders, regularly says, 'A Sunday

experience that focuses on welcoming people isn't a threat to your faith, it's an opportunity for your faith.' However, in the Church we often want to create the divide between sacred and secular. The world likes us to keep our church stuff in our church buildings, but the church often seems like it's just as happy to keep the world out and batten down the hatches! Is it just too scary out there? Are we afraid of who might come through the doors if we opened them just a little wider?

When I was a child, we used to sing a song in Sunday school called *Jesus Bids Us Light* (written in 1868 by Susan Bogert Warner – and no, I'm not that old). To be honest, I sang it with no idea what the words meant. Now, as I look back at this theologically inaccurate song, I have a problem with its lyrics:

> *Jesus bids us shine,*
> *With a pure, clear light,*
> *Like a little candle,*
> *Burning in the night.*
> *In this world is darkness,*
> *So let us shine –*
> *You in your small corner,*
> *And I in mine.*

The basic idea is that we live in a world that is a dark, dark place, and that you and I, as followers of Jesus Christ, are like little candles – and if we shine our light, we will affect the darkness around us. If you sit in your small corner and I in mine, we will take the world for Jesus.

But the reality is that 'the world' and 'church' should not be defined as two totally separate entities. In Jesus' prayer for His followers in John 17, He suggests that we are called to be in the world (v18), but not belong to it (v14), and in Matthew 10 He encourages His disciples to be 'as shrewd as snakes and harmless as doves' (v16) when we go into this world. To define people by whether they are 'in the world' or 'in the church' would be irrational and unbiblical. We are called to engage with the needs of our world, not try to remove ourselves from it.

This is not a world full of worldly people and churches stuffed with churchy people. There are simply *people*, and as far as God is concerned, they are all people He has made and they really matter to Him. And it's not just today's Church that needs reminding of this. Paul wrote to the church in Galatia and reminded them that:

> There is no longer Jew or Gentile, slave or free, male and female. For you are all one in Christ Jesus.
> Galatians 3:28

The church is for *all people* – regardless of age, gender, sexuality, race, culture, wealth, status or even 'churched' and '0unchurched'.

People really matter

The story of Jesus kicking out the Temple traders (Matt. 21) is often used to argue that shopping on a Sunday is wrong, even though we don't know which day of the week this happened on. But the financial transactions taking place weren't what upset Jesus – it was the way that the Temple was designed to limit access to people who did not 'fit in'. The Temple was built with specific areas: the holy of holies for the priests, the inner court for the able-bodied male Jews, and the outer courts where women and children were allowed. Disabled people and people of other nations and religions would not be allowed into the outer court. Jewish women and children were not allowed into the inner court, and Jewish men were not allowed into the holy of holies if they were not a Levitical priest. It was this system of segregation that Jesus was frustrated by. See what happened after Jesus knocked over the tables:

> Jesus entered the Temple and began to drive out all the people buying and selling animals for sacrifice. He knocked over the tables of the money changers and the chairs of those selling doves. He said to them, 'The Scriptures declare, "My Temple will be called a house of prayer," but you have turned it into a den of thieves!'
> The blind and the lame came to him in the Temple, and he healed them. The leading priests and the teachers of religious law saw these wonderful miracles and heard even the children in the Temple shouting, 'Praise God for the Son of David.'
> But the leaders were indignant. They asked Jesus, 'Do you hear what these children are saying?'
> 'Yes,' Jesus replied. 'Haven't you ever read the Scriptures? For they say, "You have taught children and infants to give you praise."' Then he returned to Bethany, where he stayed overnight.
> Matthew 21:12–17

The blind and the lame came into the Temple; the children started to sing in the Temple. Jesus had created access to all areas for all people. This is the desire of Jesus: that all people can come in and be at one with His Father.

Generally, it's very easy to like people who are like us, or people we aspire to be like, but we need to work harder at getting to know people who are different to us. As Abraham Lincoln famously said, 'I don't like that man. I must get to know him better.' The challenge is always not to treat people how we see them, but to ask God how He sees them. To give you an example of where this hasn't happened: one Sunday, before church started, a member of our welcome team came to see me to let me know that we had some visitors. They then whispered in my ear that this new couple were 'unmarried' and 'living together'. Staying calm, I asked this person if they knew our visitors' names – but unfortunately, although they knew their marital status and living arrangements, they hadn't discovered their *names*. By far, the most important and wonderful thing was that these two people had come to our church that day – everything else should be secondary. Would they have been 'more welcome' if they were already married?

In his book *No Perfect People Allowed*, John Burke talks about teaching his church to give up trying to fix people:

> It's not our job – that's God's job. Instead, seek to accept and love people in order to reconnect them with God... This doesn't mean you never point out sinful or destructive behavior, but you don't focus on it.[7]

People are more important than their labels. We mustn't try to 'fix' people, but welcome them into our churches with open arms, endeavour to get to know them for who they are and allow the Holy Spirit, in His own timing, to gently work in their lives as they encounter God for themselves.

Everyone being welcome in church has to be more than just a slogan. We need to be hospitable and welcoming churches, open and accessible for all. It's not about trying to be slick, but welcoming. It's not about creating a machine, but creating a community.

Encounter needs a language

Despite the many hours we might spend trying to come up with church vision statements, mission declarations and lists of values, the mission of the Church hasn't changed since Jesus gave the great commission:

> Jesus came and told his disciples, 'I have been given all authority in heaven and on earth. Therefore, go and make disciples of all the nations, baptizing them in the name of the Father and the Son and the Holy Spirit. Teach these new disciples to obey all the commands I have given you. And be sure of this: I am with you always, even to the end of the age.'
> Matthew 28:18–20

It's pretty simple: we are called to go and make disciples, baptising and teaching them. Yes, our churches need to be welcoming to all, but our purpose does not stop there. We don't welcome you so that you get comfortable and stay seated. We welcome you in so you can encounter God and become His disciple, and then go make more disciples and baptise them. I really believe this needs to be more normal than it is. Churches seem to live in fear of losing the handful of people that they do have rather than empowering and releasing their congregation to go into all the nations.

Just in case we weren't absolutely sure that Jesus meant what He said, He underlined His great commission with some amazing final words to His followers before ascending back to heaven. We love to quote famous people's last words and tend to place great stock on the amassed wisdom in those final breaths, but these are the last words of the death-conquering, world-changing Son of God who is levitating back to heaven accompanied by angels... so we should probably take note:

> But you will receive power when the Holy Spirit comes
> upon you. And you will be my witnesses, telling people
> about me everywhere—in Jerusalem, throughout Judea,
> in Samaria, and to the ends of the earth.
> Acts 1:8

We need to be filled with the Holy Spirit and tell people *everywhere*. We can start locally, in our own hometowns, but that's not where it stops – we need to get going to the ends of the earth before we take a break (and Jesus was not simply being metaphorical or poetic when He said that).

In our desire to be welcoming and accessible, we must never think that creating a comfortable and hospitable environment is, in and of itself, the mission of the Church. It is merely a potential starting point to enable people to meet and encounter God for themselves. The last thing we want is for church to become a consumerist event, with a comfortable seat and some corporate singing to make us all feel a little better about our weekly efforts in fulfilling Jesus' final words. We need to be authentic, contagious communities that express the power of God in all of our activities so that through our very welcome they see something of God Himself. The gospel message is not something that needs tidying up or dumbing down for people who don't yet know God. In fact, we need to ensure that we don't create such a smooth and slick Sunday presentation that the very power of God gets lost to those listening.

> For Christ didn't send me to baptize, but to preach the
> Good News—and not with clever speech, for fear that the
> cross of Christ would lose its power.
> 1 Corinthians 1:17

Sometimes we need to get out of the way so that people can experience the full power of God, and His mission can be accomplished. We need to mind our language – a lot of 'Christianese' makes us needlessly sound weird. Asking a newcomer to your church if they are 'washed in the blood of the Lamb' sounds a little off-putting, to say the least. But we also need to make sure that we don't 'dumb down' or reduce the gospel message to something so palatable that it loses its power. If people come to church looking for God, they will be disappointed if all they find is a tidy presentation. They need to hear the story of God, His love for them and His desire to be reconnected to His lost children: how He gave up all that He had, His Son Jesus, to die on a cross that we could all be saved and come into a new relationship with our Father God.

Jesus never set out to confuse or alienate people with His teaching, but used simple storytelling – parables – to make His point in a relatable and memorable way. He didn't talk down to people, but used language that got through to them. Children were welcome. Tax collectors were welcome. The disgraced prodigal son, smelling strongly of the pigs that he had been feeding when he came to his senses, was welcomed home.

Everyone's welcome, because that's God's way.

Yet sometimes our language suggests the opposite.

> And if someone asks about your hope as a believer,
> always be ready to explain it. But do this in a gentle and
> respectful way.
> 1 Peter 3:15–16

Just as we can disengage people with the wrong language, we can put people off with the wrong attitude. How many of us have got caught up in a theological debate, focused on being right or getting our point across, with so much zeal that we've forgotten to be 'gentle' and 'respectful'? Maybe we've got the 'always be ready to explain' part, but need to work on our timing and presentation skills as we stay in tune with the Spirit.

When it comes to our public church meetings, we need to watch our language – and not just when it comes to our theology. If we want our churches to be accessible so that everyone can experience God, then we need to take time to explain to any potential guests what we are doing so that they feel at home.

I recently visited a church that was in the middle of a shopping complex. I arrived just as the third service of the day was starting. The hall was pitch black, so we had to quite literally find our own seats. No one welcomed us from the stage – the band just burst into songs, some of which sounded familiar, but many were new to me and I struggled to join in. When we had completed exactly 30 minutes of singing, the lights went down even more (which was quite an achievement), and a video was played with information about future events that were coming up that week. It was obvious that the people on the video were talking to the regulars in the church who knew the language. Then, just as suddenly, the video stopped, a spotlight focused on a lectern on the stage and a guy started speaking to us without introducing himself. A friend who was with me tried to help me understand what he was saying, but it was hard to follow. After exactly 30 minutes of talking was over, everyone rushed out to the safety of the coffee bar to talk with their friends that they knew. Hardly anyone came to speak to me, and I wandered out into the sunshine wondering what I had just experienced.

To be fair, this particular church was in the city of Cherkasy in Ukraine and very few people spoke English. But it did make me consider how often in our churches we speak in a language that visitors struggle to understand (and then we wonder why they don't come back for a second week). Let's never assume that because what we're doing and saying makes sense to us, it must surely be understood by others.

Encounter requires a space

God wants to meet with His people – He has been in the habit of doing it for years, often in significant spaces. In no particular order: He met Moses at a burning bush, who then built an impressive tent called the tabernacle to meet in; Solomon, with the provisions set aside from his father King David, built a temple to house the very presence of God; Noah built an altar after surviving the Flood; and Jacob set up a pillar at Bethel after physically wrestling with God. For centuries, millennia even, mankind has been creating different ways to connect with God through beautiful buildings and artistic spaces.

But God is not limited to buildings, and He never intended to be. The prophet Isaiah, in his final chapter, wrote these words:

> This is what the LORD says:
> 'Heaven is my throne,
> and the earth is my footstool.
> Could you build me a temple as good as that?
> Could you build me such a resting place?'
> Isaiah 66:1

We will never be able to build anything as magnificent as heaven itself for God. He is bigger than any building we can imagine, and Jesus is greater than any temple (Matt. 12:6) – but church can create spaces that enable us to encounter God more readily. Yes, as an individual you can encounter God behind your steering wheel as you drive your car or on your knees in the lounge, but to enable others to encounter God requires a space. When we create deliberate spaces for God's people to encounter Him, it builds expectation, reduces distraction and develops healthy habits that allow us to pause and meet with God.

It doesn't matter whether it is a tent in the wilderness, an ancient monument, a beautiful garden or a hired school hall: we have a responsibility as the Church to create spaces that will help people meet God in unique ways. When you create the right space and eliminate noise, people will encounter God in a way that is unique to them.

The art of welcome

All ministry takes place in an environment,[8] and the way we present our spaces – whether for worship or for the children's work – says something about our expectations of who is coming through the door. Our environment makes a statement about what we are expecting. And what we expect and prepare for, we are more likely to experience.

When we're expecting guests at home, most of us would tidy up (or at least hide the mess!) before they arrive, and get the good biscuits out (maybe even displayed beautifully on a plate if making the extra effort). You would welcome them in, take their coat, point out the toilet if they needed it, offer them some refreshments and then find some comfortable seats and introduce them to other members of your family. Yet when it comes to the house of God, we might give a polite nod to the guest as they enter the building and hope they work it out for themselves – or just hope they have the ability to ask other people for help in where to find things.

It's worth repeating: always welcome people. It might be their first time or their hundredth time. Still welcome them. If regulars get high fives, hugs and screams of delight and first-time guests get a polite handshake and an uncomfortable stare (or worse, a look over the shoulder for someone more interesting who might be arriving) they will feel unwelcome. Train those on the welcome team to welcome people with eye contact before they have even got to the door and find out straight away if it is their first time at church. Make them feel at home. If it is their first time, that team member must take responsibility to explain how church works on a Sunday, show them how to book in their children if required, point out toilets, find them some suitable seats and introduce them to other people who are waiting for the meeting to start.

Names are important

Introducing yourself by name is powerful: it starts the conversation and establishes a mutual relationship. I once met a well-known author and church leader at a conference, and in our conversation, I realised that we did not live that far apart and enquired whether we could catch up over a coffee sometime. His response? 'Google me.'

Yup. Amazing. Needless to say, we never did get that coffee, but I have never forgotten that conversation.

Learn new people's names and use them regularly. People want to be *known*. Rick Warren, Senior Pastor at Saddleback Community Church in California, says he knew everyone in the congregation by name until they exceeded 1,000 members.[9] I struggle to remember the names of my own family sometimes…

But not only should we introduce ourselves in our conversations, we should also introduce ourselves when we are participating in a church service. If you are leading the church meeting, then introduce yourself and explain what you are doing. It won't take long, and you will make people feel at home. Thank the worship team by name (unless you have a 100-piece orchestra), introduce the person preaching, celebrate those who participate and use their names – it gives them value. Jesus always had time for people and called them by name; we should as well.

Familiarity

One of the biggest traps we can fall into with language is familiarity. It's easy to assume that people know what we are talking about, but that creates a separation between 'them' and 'us' – those who are in and those who are out. We do it in our workplaces with acronyms, we do it in our families with nicknames for each other, and we do it in our churches. We assume that people know who someone is or what role they play. We mention someone's spouse, but don't give their name. It can be endearing to the visitor as it shows there is a great sense of community, but it can also make people feel like they are on the outside looking in.

In-house jokes or too much friendly banter can also be unhelpful. (This is one I have to personally continue to work on.) I may introduce a well-known preacher in our church and then make a joke at their expense. The person I am introducing may find it funny, but those listening may not understand the level of our relationship and may think I'm being disrespectful. This is also a challenge within a diverse society such as the UK, where there are often a variety of cultures represented. What may be humorous to one culture might be completely lost on another. When I travel, even to other nations that speak English, I have to think carefully about any jokes I may use as part of my preach. We may speak the same language, but we are not always saying the same thing.

Let's also be careful when making references to previous experiences. 'Remember Margaret at last year's church weekend talent night? Comedy gold.' Hilarious for those who were there and remember Margaret dressing up and doing an uncanny impression of Kylie Minogue – absolutely meaningless to everyone else.

The same is also true of church announcements or notices – having a Bible study and a bacon roll at Betty's sounds lovely, but who is Betty and where does she live? Again, these moments in a church can express something of the diversity and delight of the community in the church, but it can also remind those visiting that they are not yet part of this family and it isn't all that clear how they might start to join in.

Preaching

Sometimes people say that we must not 'dumb down' Scripture for those who are new to faith or first-time guests, and I completely agree. But if you are a preacher, your job is to communicate the Bible in a powerful and effective way. If people are bored or excluded because they do not understand the Word of God, then we are not doing our job properly. To communicate simply, we must understand profoundly.

We've touched on this already, but it bears repeating: using the longest and fanciest words we possibly can in a bid to sound eloquent might impress those who understand, but it limits other people's ability to connect and encounter God for themselves.

It is possible to communicate effectively in a way that does not exclude people who are not familiar with church language – it just takes a little more work. For instance, if we say to those meeting on a Sunday to 'turn to John', the regulars will all know to turn to the book in the Bible known as the Gospel of John... but the average person who has never been to church before will be looking around the room for someone called John! We can easily get around this as communicators by saying, 'In the Bible, there are four books known as the Gospels, which tell the good news story about Jesus and His life here on earth. The fourth one was written by a man called John, and we are going to read from that book today.' Yes, it has taken you an extra sentence to explain, but no one is excluded, and people will feel more comfortable in what might already be an alien experience for many.

Never assume that people know their way around the Bible. We now live in a world where very few people have had a traditional 'Sunday school upbringing' and have an understanding of how the Bible is structured or what the various genres within it are. People may not know that the Bible is not just one book but many books, and they may have no idea about the difference between the Old Testament and New Testament, let alone know the difference between the various writers who contributed to this incredible document that is both ancient and alive. It is our responsibility to explain and teach Scripture and never assume. It takes more effort to explain, but preaching is not about impressing others with your knowledge of Scripture. It's about helping those listening to encounter God for themselves through His Word.

In the same way that the best script writers aren't always the best actors, the best theologians don't always make the best preachers. Work with others who have different skills to teach the Bible clearly and with great understanding. As Spurgeon famously said, preaching the Bible is like letting the lion out of the cage.[10] Let's preach it well and allow the power that is in the ancient words to affect those listening.

In the Early Church, the apostles took this role very seriously. They made it a key part of their work and didn't want to be distracted from it, so they appointed others to care for those in the community that were in need (Acts 6:1–7). Although the local community that the apostles were preaching to would have had a good understanding of the Old Testament and Jewish law, they would have had little understanding of the message of Jesus and that He was fulfilling that same law. The Early Church preachers had to be creative in how they taught a society that had rejected Jesus, so we need to do likewise.

Sung worship

At the very core of our being is a desire to worship the one who made us, but how we do that differs across the world with many traditions arising over centuries. Why do we, in the Western Church, generally sing songs and call that 'worship', as if singing is all worship is?

I remember hosting a service where our guest speaker was a Methodist minister. At the start of the meeting he turned to me and asked, 'When do you want me to preach?' and I replied, 'After the worship.' As I said this, he looked very confused and I realised my error. For a Methodist, the whole meeting is a time of worship – not just the singing part – which is arguably more accurate. We talk about worship songs, worship leaders, worship bands... but our worship is so much more than singing a few songs on a Sunday. It is every breath that we take, acknowledging the God who made us; it is admiring the beauty of creation; the opportunity to be still and sit in silence. It is our kindness to someone who is struggling, our attitude to others in the traffic jam we find ourselves in, our generous giving to the homeless person on the street and the gracious attitude we show to those who frustrate us. All of this is worship to God.

Having said all that, many churches sing songs on a Sunday and call that 'the worship' – and it is biblical to do so.

In his letter to the Ephesians, Paul encourages us to:

> be filled with the Spirit, singing psalms and hymns and
> spiritual songs among yourselves, and making music to the
> Lord in your hearts. And give thanks for everything to God
> the Father in the name of our Lord Jesus Christ.
> Ephesians 5:18–20

But do we create moments for people to encounter God through these songs? Are the songs that we sing simply what's popular at the time, or are they the right songs to lead us into a place of deeper connection with our indescribable God?

When I was a teenager, we used to have what my friends and I called 'Bingo Sunday'. This was back when we had songbooks (before even the wondrous overhead projector had been invented), and anyone could call out the number of their favourite song, and the person on piano would turn to that song and we would all sing it together. These were some great moments – especially when people wouldn't even call out a number first and just go off-piste and start singing in whatever key they fancied. The pianist and a few brave souls would try to join in while my friends and I would try to keep our giggling to a minimum.

It seems to me that many of the churches and events that I attend have gone to the other extreme, with zero audience participation in song selection. I'm not saying there's anything wrong with a set list prepared and rehearsed in advance, but I do believe the role of worship leader is so much more than leading a band of musicians. If you are responsible for leading sung worship in your church, you're there to help everyday people, from all walks of life and facing all kinds of challenges, to connect with God Himself. Be flexible and see what God might do with a willing servant. Still make plans, still rehearse and perfect the gift God has given you, but be prepared to lay it all down in a moment if He asks you to.

Perfection is not success. Songs being sung and played perfectly is not success. Getting every intro nailed is not success. Finishing exactly on time to cue the preacher is not success. Having the best worship band in town is not success. God's people encountering Him – now that is success.

According to the Westminster Catechism of 1647, 'Man's chief end is to glorify God, and to enjoy Him forever.' Our mission is to share the good news, but our priority is to worship God.

Prayer

Prayer is simply being with God, speaking with Him and listening to Him. Prayer shouldn't be about working our way through a list of demands, but simply spending time with God – encountering Him. Yes, prayer is powerful and can make a huge difference to people's lives, and God answers our prayers for help. But prayer is not meant to be a transactional, vending machine activity: 'Prayer is like oil in a generator. You only have to be a little short on oil and the generator will fall apart.'[11]

Encountering God through prayer needs to be part of our corporate habit and our personal rhythm. Prayer is the opportunity for us, at any moment, to connect with God.

People connect with God by praying in all sorts of different ways. For some it is silence; for others it is walking the dog at sunset; for some it is driving the car with the music up loud. For some it is liturgical and repetitive; for others it is creative and different every day. I love the fact that, in my town, the local churches pray in different ways. The parish church, Romsey Abbey, is always open for people to come in and pray. You can sit quietly, light a candle and encounter God gently. The Methodist Church in our town prays for a different street each week. They drop a letter into that particular road to let them know they are praying and then advertise outside their church which lane, street or road they are praying for.

For those of us who lead times of corporate prayer, maybe we need to rethink how we do so. Let's make it part of our weekly church services, not as a task that has to be completed, but as an opportunity for encounter, not to be missed.

Communion

One of the ways in which the Early Church regularly and routinely encountered God was to remember Him through the re-enactment of the last supper. This is often referred to as the Eucharist or Communion. All my life I have been part of the non-denominational Church, but my experience of taking of communion has often been fairly solemn. I remember the little squares of bread that were carefully prepared, the shiny wooden carrying tray with a handle in the middle that would hold all the little glasses of blackcurrant squash, and the holes in the back of the chairs where we would put our glasses once we had finished. (Ironically, I was recently at a wedding reception where the evening bar staff were using pretty much the exact same tray to deliver and collect shot glasses.)

While a certain amount of structure and logistical planning is helpful for taking communion in a church environment, we need to be careful that we don't take what should be a celebration meal with friends and turn it into a mere tradition, void of all encounter. That was never the idea when Jesus said to His disciples to 'Do this in remembrance of me' (1 Cor. 11:23–26). I believe Jesus was saying that whenever we get together with family, friends and followers to eat, we should remember Him.

Lottie and I were once invited to the home of a preacher for dinner. Before we started the meal, our friend poured a glass of red wine and placed it in the middle of the table. My wife Lottie took hold of the glass, raised it up and said, 'Cheers!' to our hosts. They looked a little surprised, and then pointed out that before we ate together we were going to take communion – something they did every mealtime. Lottie was more than a little embarrassed, while I was just relieved that it wasn't me who had taken the glass (though I did give her the 'I can't believe you just did that!' look). Although this is not our normal habit, I loved the idea that, for this couple, it was part of their everyday mealtime and not just part of their Sunday service.

The writer of the book of Acts makes it clear that the Early Church took communion in their homes, as well as sharing meals together, and they did it with great joy and generosity – a challenge to all of us. We could do with a lot more fun and joy in the church. I recently heard about a church that had set themselves a challenge to host 100 parties in 50 days as a way of connecting with their local community. I love this.

Maybe, if we want to encounter God in our homes more, we need to take time when we eat together with our families and friends, to pause and to take communion so that we can truly 'do this in remembrance of Him'.

Encountering God is not always about the national festivals and the big moments. It can be in the stillness and the quiet, or in the middle of the storm. Elijah encountered God not in the wind, earthquake or fire, but in the gentle whisper (1 Kings 19:11–13). If we want to encounter God for ourselves and hear Him whisper, we need to learn to pause what we are doing, lean in and listen for what He wants to say.

I believe anyone can encounter God and, although this will be unique to each one of us, I believe that the Church when it gathers is one of the greatest opportunities for us to experience and encounter God in a fresh way. None of it matters unless there has been an encounter.

Gather

Together is
always better

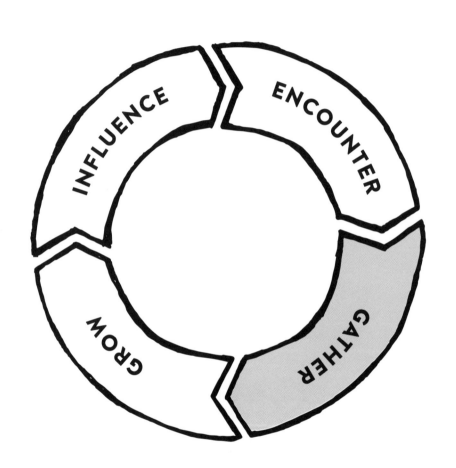

Gather starts on Sunday (usually...)

> Let us think of ways to motivate one another to acts of
> love and good works. And let us not neglect our meeting
> together, as some people do, but encourage one another,
> especially now that the day of his return is drawing near.
> Hebrews 10:24–25

I still believe in the importance of the gathered Church. Many writers have suggested that the church service or gathering has had its day; that we need to be dispersed into the community and 'be the Church' wherever we find ourselves; that we need to be 'empowering the disciples' and not just 'paying the pastors'. Now, I completely agree with these suggestions and recognise that we as the Church are perhaps guilty of becoming too focused on church attendance, judging our performance based on how many people turn up – but there is strength in getting together as the people of God. It is a healthy spiritual habit and not something we should dismiss as low priority.

If we never get together as Christians, then we tend to disappear more than disperse. Our getting together can keep us on track and keep us healthy as followers of Christ. If we never get together, how can we have a safe place for people to come and find us, whatever their story, background or disappointments? Are they just meant to walk around our local high street and wave a flag in the hope that we find them? (Having said that, let's remember that our ultimate purpose is not hanging around all together at the weekends in a safe bubble of Christianity. It's a chance to be built up, challenged, taught, ministered to and then sent out and scattered to be the Church in the world in which we live between each Sunday.)

Stuart Bell, leader of Alive Church, Lincoln and founder of the Ground Level Network of Churches, uses the phrase, 'When we gather, we are assembled.' I firmly believe that we need to be built up as followers of Jesus before we are sent out as scattered servants on a mission.

Throughout the Bible, the people of God gathered for many reasons. In the Old Testament, Israel gathered for an incredible variety of festivals and feasts, gathering to remember their past and to make and renew covenants, as well as gathering regularly for times of worship (often documented throughout the Psalms[12]). But in the New Testament, Jesus took the gathering to a whole new level. It seemed that wherever He went, people gathered to Him to listen to His teaching. When Jesus preached, crowds assembled expecting something extraordinary, and they weren't disappointed: thousands fed with a small boy's packed lunch; a man lowered through the ceiling by his friends and then healed; a makeshift floating pulpit by using a fishing boat.

After Jesus ascended to heaven in Acts 1, the first thing His followers did was gather together in the upper room. Then, in Acts 2, the Holy Spirit turned up in an incredible way and transformed them as a gathered community to become what would be known as the Early Church. This group then gathered daily, to experience the miracles of God, to break bread and eat together, and receive teaching from the apostles.

I believe a biblical church consists of believers coming together in the same physical space to gather and worship (Matt. 18:20). If you are not gathering, you are not a church. We gather to respond to God's invitation to be part of His family. Our thought should never be, 'Shall I go this week?' or 'Can I be bothered this morning?', but 'Let's go to church – what an amazing opportunity to enter the presence of God.'

> Hearing this, a man sitting at the table with Jesus exclaimed, 'What a blessing it will be to attend a banquet in the Kingdom of God!'
> Jesus replied with this story: 'A man prepared a great feast and sent out many invitations. When the banquet was ready, he sent his servant to tell the guests, "Come, the banquet is ready." But they all began making excuses. One said, "I have just bought a field and must inspect it. Please excuse me." Another said, "I have just bought five pairs of oxen, and I want to try them out. Please excuse me." Another said, "I just got married, so I can't come."
> The servant returned and told his master what they had said. His master was furious and said, "Go quickly into the streets and alleys of the town and invite the poor, the crippled, the blind, and the lame." After the servant had done this, he reported, "There is still room for more." So his master said, "Go out into the country lanes and behind the hedges and urge anyone you find to come, so that the house will be full. For none of those I first invited will get even the smallest taste of my banquet."'
> Luke 14:15–24

When Jesus told this parable, He gave examples of the excuses that many people still use today: 'We have relatives coming for lunch' or 'We have work to prepare for Monday'. There might be many very real reasons why we can't get to church every single week, but we do usually have a choice as to whether or not we are gathering with other Christians. If we're really honest with ourselves, we probably could get up a bit earlier and get our work done, or invite our relatives to church with us. God has something amazing prepared for us when we gather, so let's make it a priority.

At Freedom Church we don't have members, we have partners. (I think I borrowed the idea from the John Lewis group who call their employees 'partners'). In our church, a partner is someone who participates in the church with their time, treasure and talents. Some of this we will cover in later chapters, but the first element, time, reveals our commitment to our church community. When we turn up regularly it expresses to those around us that we are committed to them and the church family that we form together. We all have colleagues in our workplaces that say they are committed to the business, but then always seem to be the last person to arrive at meetings or offer to help when there is a need. Attendance is an expression of our commitment. I can tell my wife I am committed to her, but if I rarely go home she might question my commitment! I believe we need to encourage the habit of attending church, even when we don't want to or it's not convenient. I'm not saying we need to become legalistic and attend every single church meeting regardless of other pressures, but let's not allow our non-attendance to be for insignificant reasons (that perhaps reveal our true priorities). What I mean is, if we have chosen to give our lives to following Jesus, then everything changes and He has priority – always.

Sometimes, it's a real battle getting to church – physically (getting out of bed!), spiritually, mentally, emotionally and relationally – and at times, our commitment to church might feel like a costly and sacrificial slog. But our obedience in turning up, joining in and contributing to the community of God isn't just about showing God or other people that we are 'good Christians'. Church benefits us, too, in immeasurable ways. Gathering together is often a great place for us to recalibrate. Sometimes we go off-track, make poor decisions, or start to drift away from what God would want for us. When we gather and declare the truth about who God is – when we listen afresh to the Bible, the very words of God, and receive from Him, it's like hitting the reset button. Meeting with God and His people regularly keeps us accountable, encouraged and energised. Why wouldn't we want that every week?! Sure, we can download a podcast of the talk and listen to a worship playlist (both great things to do), but it's never quite the same as the joy that comes from being with others and encountering God together. That's the wonderful thing about all this 'togetherness' – we're not supposed to do this whole faith thing on our own:

> Stay alert! Watch out for your great enemy, the devil.
> He prowls around like a roaring lion, looking for
> someone to devour.
> 1 Peter 5:8

Notice the word 'someone'. Our enemy's strategy is not to wipe out a massive group of people, but to pick us off, one at a time. Most predators will aim at prey who have wandered away from the pack. The devil looks to devour an individual – a 'someone' to finish off – and he is on the prowl.

It amazes me how often I speak to people who have not been at church for a while, and they tell me that they 'need a little me-time' or they are facing some difficult challenges so they 'want to be on their own while they work it out'. Someone else recently said to me, 'I only attended church because I was struggling with something, but now I am fine so there is no need to attend.' Relying on ourselves is the worst way to grow as a Christian. Even Jesus, the Son of God, found Himself some travel companions for His years of ministry. They may not have always been the best prayer buddies (often sleeping on the job), but they were an assorted bunch of misfits who He chose to share His life with. How much more do *we* need each other! If we are struggling with life, let's push into our church community and find God in the crowd, not in the dark corner of our bedroom where we are in danger of becoming an easy meal for a prowling lion.

We are stronger together as the church of God, and when we gather and declare God's truth and hear stories of God's goodness in people's lives, our faith increases and something changes inside us. When we gather, there is a connection between each individual and heaven itself. We join with the angels as we celebrate our God, the King of kings. The ultimate party.

When we look back at those ten characteristics of the Early Church, we can see that they regularly met together in one place (Acts 2:44). It was a vital part of their spiritual habit that helped pioneer and shape this earliest Christian community. When we recommit ourselves to the simple principle of turning up to gather together, let's see what happens – both in the church community and in our hearts.

The power of belonging

Church leader Simon Benham likens some churches to peaches and coconuts. He suggests a peach is easy to get into and solid at the core, while a coconut is hard to get into and disappointing in the centre.[13] If we're really honest, are our churches more focused on people's behaviour than making them feel like they belong? The desire to belong is in each one of us – it is what makes us human.

As we have said before, when the Church works right, it is the most amazing community to be a part of. Every week I hear stories of people in our church giving people lifts, offering to help people financially, babysitting, sending gifts, taking people out for meals or coffee, giving flowers, helping people move house, visiting those in hospital, inviting people round for a cup of tea, taking part in fundraising activities for the church and other charities.... People are amazing. All around the world, in every style of church and denomination, often without any co-ordination or pressure from the leader, Christians are expressing God's love in a variety of ways. The Church when it gathers to serve is amazing.

But what often begins as simply church – a group of people who love Jesus and want to live life His way – becomes complicated (and often without our realising it). We grow too big for the home we meet in, so now we need to hire a hall. If we hire a hall, we will need some money... and we will also need someone to unlock it and clean it and set it up, someone to welcome people, and someone to ensure those attending can hear and see everything clearly. We have some families join us with children, so we want to look after them – and we need to do it properly with safeguarding, data protection and appropriate training.

All of this is true, necessary and important – but the danger is that before we know it, this beautiful community of Jesus followers drifts into becoming event managers, legal experts and childcare specialists, all wondering why they feel so exhausted.

This is not just true of churches, but of all organisations. In her book *A Simpler Way*, organisational expert Margaret Wheatley puts it like this:

most people have a desire to love their organizations...
They fall in love with the identity that is trying to be
expressed... But then we take this vital passion and
institutionalize it. We create an organization... Passion
mutates into procedure, into rules and roles. Instead of
purpose, we focus on policies. Instead of being free to
create, we impose constraints that squeeze the life out
of us. The organization no longer lives. We see its bloated
form and resent it for what it stops us from doing.[14]

Simple becomes complex. The opposite of what we hoped for.

But if we take time to consider – really consider – what we do, there are ways to communicate the complex in a simple way. The best teachers and scientists can take an incredibly intricate theory and communicate them in such a way that school children can understand and be inspired by them. The local church is often guilty of plodding on in its growing complexity, expecting newcomers to just 'get it' or work it out for themselves, rather than creating clear pathways for new believers or first-time church attenders.

I have regularly made this mistake. If you are involved in church leadership or part of the organisational structure for your church, you can easily assume that everyone is part of your conversations (including the ones that happen in your head!), and can be surprised when someone questions why you have made the latest changes.

It's also very easy to keep adding to the church programme without ever stopping another church activity. A successful church is not a busy church. Busyness is not effectiveness. Doing less but doing it well is always more effective. Making the decision to take a break from an activity, or knowing when something has run its course, is really important. This is why we need to work hard as local church communities to keep things simple, and continually remind ourselves of why we are doing what we are doing: because *God loves us*, and wants us to show others that love.

Better together

On the eve of His arrest, Jesus prayed an amazing prayer for His followers to have unity:

> Now I am coming to you. I told them many things while I was with them in this world so they would be filled with my joy. I have given them your word. And the world hates them because they do not *belong* to the world, just as I do not *belong* to the world. I'm not asking you to take them out of the world, but to keep them safe from the evil one. They do not *belong* to this world any more than I do. Make them holy by your truth; teach them your word, which is truth. Just as you sent me into the world, I am sending them into the world. And I give myself as a holy sacrifice for them so they can be made holy by your truth.
> I am praying not only for these disciples but also for all who will ever believe in me through their message. I pray that they will all be one, just as you and I are one—as you are in me, Father, and I am in you. And may they be in us so that the world will believe you sent me.
> I have given them the glory you gave me, so they may be one as we are one. I am in them and you are in me. May they experience such perfect *unity* that the world will know that you sent me and that you love them as much as you love me. Father, I want these whom you have given me to be with me where I am. Then they can see all the

> glory you gave me because you loved me even before the world began!
> O righteous Father, the world doesn't know you, but I do; and these disciples know you sent me. I have revealed you to them, and I will continue to do so. Then your love for me will be in them, and I will be in them.
> John 17:13–26 (emphasis added)

Jesus wanted us to be one as He and the Father were one. In a lonely society where people crave to belong, the Church can and should be a place where true community can be created – where people can be part of a family and belong to one another, knowing their true value as sons and daughters of God.

We have all been designed to have a need to connect with other people. When God created Adam, he said it was not good for him to be alone (Gen. 2:18). I'm guessing that there might be a whole load of reasons for that! We are created to exist in community. We all need to know that somebody can empathise with what we are feeling and understand something of who we are. Many people would love to be connected back to their Father God and part of a local church, but they just don't know how or where to start.

Ideally, churches should be diverse communities with many ages and demographics represented, joined together by their love for God. But in modern Western society, particularly in recent years, the local church has become even more diverse, often with multiple nationalities and cultures coming together. Some people will quickly feel included and at home; others will feel uncomfortable with the singing of songs to Jesus, or the awkward conversation over tea and biscuits, or the way Bob on the door gives everyone a hug of welcome. Some will feel included and part of the church; others will feel like they are on the outside of the community looking in.

And often, it's the people who are assumed by others to feel included, who actually feel very much left out (and vice versa). It amazes me how often I can be talking to one of the seemingly 'in crowd' people, and they tell me how lonely they are, or that they don't quite feel like they belong.

You may have heard it said that friendship is a lot like food: we need it to survive. What's more, we have a basic drive for it. Psychologists find that human beings have a fundamental need for inclusion in group life and for close relationships. Community is so important. It is the opposite of loneliness, and loneliness is one our biggest and often unseen killers in society. It's a fact that we are healthier in community than we are alone (even though it often means we catch each other's colds). We need each other. We need to be connected.

In the book of Romans, the writer Paul comes up with this well-known concept of us having different parts to play in community. He absolutely nails this idea of belonging – that as the Church, we all belong to each other:

> Because of the privilege and authority God has given
> me, I give each of you this warning: Don't think you are
> better than you really are. Be honest in your evaluation of
> yourselves, measuring yourselves by the faith God has given
> us. Just as our bodies have many parts and each part has
> a special function, so it is with Christ's body. We are many
> parts of one body, and we all belong to each other.
> In his grace, God has given us different gifts for doing
> certain things well. So if God has given you the ability to
> prophesy, speak out with as much faith as God has given
> you. If your gift is serving others, serve them well. If you are
> a teacher, teach well. If your gift is to encourage others, be

> encouraging. If it is giving, give generously. If God has given
> you leadership ability, take the responsibility seriously. And
> if you have a gift for showing kindness to others, do it gladly.
> Don't just pretend to love others. Really love them. Hate
> what is wrong. Hold tightly to what is good. Love each
> other with genuine affection, and take delight in honoring
> each other. Never be lazy, but work hard and serve the Lord
> enthusiastically. Rejoice in our confident hope. Be patient
> in trouble, and keep on praying. When God's people are in
> need, be ready to help them. Always be eager to practice
> hospitality.
> Romans 12:3–13

There is so much truth and wisdom in this passage, and it's a timely warning for us today: don't think of yourself as being bigger or better than you are, but play your part by being humble and bringing the gift that God has given you. We need to get a healthy perspective from God on who we are and what each of us contribute to this thing called Church. It's a stark reminder that mirrors what Jesus said in Matthew's Gospel: 'those who exalt themselves will be humbled, and those who humble themselves will be exalted' (Matt. 23:12).

Paul develops this way of thinking in a number of his letters, using this metaphor of us being one body. It is a helpful picture, though maybe a little weird if we overthink it (you may enjoy *The Message* version of Romans 12 in particular: 'as a chopped-off finger or cut-off toe we wouldn't amount to much, would we?'). We need each other. Everyone plays their part. We all have something to contribute and we are better together.

Of course, we'll sometimes face the challenge of more than one person wanting to carry out the same role, or, perhaps more commonly, a need for a volunteer but no one willing or able.

I genuinely believe that God will provide all our needs when it comes to people and the parts we play. When I meet new people in our church I try to ask the question, 'What is the gift that you bring with you?' rather than saying, 'We have a desperate need for a bass guitarist – you'd better start learning to play, as you're in the band next Sunday.' I believe God brings people into our church communities to use the gifts that He has already given to them. And if we don't have the gifts available, then I am comfortable leaving those vacancies in place until the right person comes along. Square pegs don't fit in round holes, and can do some damage to the people around them. It's always better to have people working in their natural gifting and feeling like they are making a real, important contribution. We all want to be valued for who we are and what we bring. Having gaps in the volunteer rota is a tension to be managed. It's not for us to get frustrated about and force people to fill the gaps when they don't have the skill or desire.

The challenge, then, is embracing our diversity within our unity – and we can only do this by gathering regularly and connecting. When the people saw how the Early Church loved each other and shared all that they had, they were attracted to this developing community of believers.

Gather in small groups

Whether you call them connect groups, life groups, home groups, cell groups or collectives, I'm going to suggest something that might sound strange: ideally, we shouldn't really need official small group 'structures' in our churches. I like to think that, in a perfect world, we should be able to simply create community ourselves and invite others to join our activities. If you filled a room with children and some simple equipment, they would soon find ways to interact and engage with each other, but as adults, we often seem to struggle. Gathering together on a smaller and more intimate scale is an essential part of community. We've already said that a sense of belonging is crucial in church, and creating small groups is one way to help people access church community and create spaces where people can build relationships and grow in faith.

A brief history...

The idea of small groups is not a new concept. The Early Church was definitely more of a house-based movement[15] and didn't have some beautiful sanctuary or high tech auditorium to meet in (well, not for the first 300 years at least). Then, as tends to happen, a movement became a monument – and instead of being an organic community, it became a system of religion and order, and lost some of its early sense of community. If we're brutally honest, there are periods of history where the established Church became a pious, individualistic model, far removed from any template we're given in Scripture. But throughout that same history have always been movements that have promoted the importance of Christian community.

We recently celebrated 500 years since Martin Luther nailed his *95 Theses* to the door of All Saints' Church in Wittenberg[16] and started a huge shift in the Church as we know it, a schism that created the Protestant movement and enabled everyday people to engage in church in a way that they hadn't previously been able to. The value of community was celebrated once again as an important part of church life.

John Wesley, the founder of Methodism, created 'classes' that met in people's homes (after he had an encounter with God in 1738), and created 'methodical' Bible studies as a support to the parish church system. Wesley never wanted this collection of small groups to become a separate denomination, but a movement begun that grew rapidly, and in 1783 the Methodist Church was officially formed.

More recently, the house church movement of the 1970s saw people return to the idea of meeting in homes. Frustrated that the established Church seemed to be dying into insignificance, and possibly impacted by the hippie era of the 1960s and the Jesus movement, the house church movement saw small churches set up in homes, with non-traditional leaders given responsibility for these small communities.

There are a number of books that comment on the phenomena and importance of small gatherings. In his book *The Second*

Reformation, Bill Beckham talks about the need for having both the large gathering and the small group in his image of the two-winged bird of 'celebration' and 'cell' – the idea being that the local church needs to have both so that it can truly soar.[17] Writing in the 1990s, Ralph Neighbor[18] suggested we rediscover the cell church model, where groups would meet in homes like the Early Church did and follow a system of the four 'W's – welcome, witness, worship and... I can never remember the last one. I do remember being part of a small group that followed this model and although the concept was excellent, we would often have disagreements over which 'W' we were on at what point in the evening...

In *Letters to the Church*, Francis Chan talks about how he came to rethink his whole approach to church by leaving the megachurch that he had founded, and instead developing a house church network of small groups:

> I saw a few other people and me using our gifts, while thousands just came and sat in the sanctuary for an hour and a half and then went home. The way we had structured the church was stunting people's growth and the whole body was weaker for it.[19]

The church that I lead in Romsey, Hampshire started from a similar model of a small group meeting in a home in the late 1970s. It began with just six people regularly gathering for prayer. They had experienced the Holy Spirit moving in a fresh way, in a season where there was often a reticence from more established churches to encourage such activity. Having grown over the last 40 years or so, Freedom Church is no longer seen as the mysterious stranger, but very much part of the local church family.

But it started with a small group.

A small group is not just a place of building community; it is also a place of care and discipleship. It's somewhere people don't just gather to drink coffee and air their thinly-disguised complaints about the volume on Sundays, but where they can be challenged and grow in their Christian understanding. Real, life-changing learning rarely happens in large gatherings with one speaker at the front of a crowd (although it absolutely can). I really believe that the most valuable kind of learning happens around a table, over food, or in a lounge, with a drink in hand. Lifelong learning happens amongst people you know, who know you. They can challenge you and encourage you, and when life is tough, they will be there for you because you are known by the group. Just like a broader church gathering, a small group requires a commitment to turning up regularly and building relationships with each other. I love the big celebration but recognise that the benefits of belonging and growing are often best experienced in a smaller group where you are known.

Many churches offer small groups in different ways. At Freedom Church, we call them 'connect groups', as we want to encourage people to connect with God, connect with each other and, through the notes we offer from the Sunday meetings, feel connected to the weekend gatherings even if they were unable to make it. Our connect groups tend to meet in homes as that seems to be easiest for most people, but sometimes people meet in coffee shops, pubs or other neutral locations. Some groups focus on Bible study and prayer for each other, but other groups focus on a specific aspect of church life – such as the worship team, which meets weekly, or groups that focus on prayer for the church and the local community. There are also other groups that get together over their love of art and creativity, football, great coffee or those with young children.

People in the more 'traditional' connect groups would expect to have the opportunity to read the Word of God, to reflect on what has been taught from the previous Sunday and to hear about each other's weeks to pray for prophesy over them and encourage them in their faith. The leaders of those groups would have some awareness of those that attend, and raise concerns about any pastoral needs that might arise. But in the more focused groups, it is much more about common activity and belonging. Rather than following any particular teaching programme, these groups are encouraged to simply meet regularly and advertise the opportunities for others to join them (some churches call these 'missional communities'). They are not expected to keep track of those who attend, but to ensure that those who do turn up are made to feel welcome and fully at home.

Practically, people need to know how to get involved with a small group – perhaps signing up online or on a Sunday. At Freedom Church, we also encourage people to 'try before you buy'. Not every group works for everyone, but most people are too polite to say, 'I don't really feel like this group is for me, and I can't help but feel particularly uncomfortable in the time of worship when Brenda does a dance solo with her ribbon in the middle of the lounge.' Instead they either never try a group again, assuming they are all the same, or, with an intense fear of offending anyone, they continue going to the same group for years, secretly hating every moment of Brenda's high kicks, totally unaware that they could have opted out. There needs to be freedom.

Gather through service

I recently had a conversation with one of the guys in my church. He's a busy man with a young family – and a new baby on the way – in a job that's offering him more and more advancement, all while studying for an academic qualification. As if that's not enough, he's an active part of the church, and each week he and his wife open their home up to the young people of our church. And still he said this: 'How can I get more involved in the life of the church? I believe I have some skills to offer, but don't know where they would be best utilised.'

I couldn't help but be impressed by his desire to serve. Often I assume people are too busy to help and I don't want to ask more of them, but I have discovered that people love to be needed and have their skills utilised. It helps them feel like part of the community. Making a request of someone is a really positive conversation – it says that they have been seen. Each of us has something to offer, and many people connect through service, not just attendance.

Everyone has God-given gifts and talents, and service is most wonderful when offered without payment, position or profile. As part of your commitment to your church, bring your gifts and share them with others. When you hold back, whether for shyness, fear of failure or perfectionism, your community will miss out on the unique part you have to offer.

Be genuine

Don't be afraid to be the real you – even if you don't like who you are and don't think other people will like who you are. In true community, we will find out eventually. Integrity far outweighs talent. Of course, people are impressed with talent initially, but great character impresses for a lifetime. Genuine people are always more attractive than loud talkers who don't always do what they say they will do. I am always more impressed by people who are quietly consistent in serving others than those who have created five minutes of excitement through a recent activity.

Speak highly of each other

What we say about people when they are not in the room is very telling. It sends a message to those listening about what you might say about them if they were not there. We are to 'encourage each other and build each other up' (1 Thess. 5:11). To create healthy community, we need to speak well of one another consistently and constantly. It sustains community and promotes it to others around us who are watching (and people are watching us more than we realise).

Opportunity and attitude

They say churches are like helicopters, because the closer you get to them, the more you get sucked into the rotas. Again, language is important here. You might consider steering away from words like 'volunteering' and 'rota' if they sound a bit clinical or off-putting. Try to make it about doing things together in a team. Serving the church is not a nuisance to your diary, but a great opportunity to serve others and get involved.

> Offer hospitality to one another without grumbling. Each
> of you should use whatever gift you have received to
> serve others, as faithful stewards of God's grace in its
> various forms. If anyone speaks, they should do so as one
> who speaks the very words of God. If anyone serves, they
> should do so with the strength God provides, so that in all
> things God may be praised through Jesus Christ. To him be
> the glory and the power for ever and ever. Amen.
> 1 Peter 4:9–11 (NIV)

I love that image of being a faithful steward of God's grace in its various forms. When we serve others, it empowers the one doing the serving and connects them with the one in need.

Service creates a sense of ownership

My eldest son has recently bought his first car. It always amazes me how much he loves his car compared to his bedroom. Most weekends he will be out on the driveway, washing and 'detailing' his car... while his bedroom remains very much unloved. Why does his car get so much more attention? He owns it. Therefore, it compels him to service.

A sense of belonging and commitment to our churches ought to compel us in a similar way. Another interesting thing about service is that it also helps people move from the outer ring of 'crowd', to the 'congregation' attending on a Sunday, to the 'core' at the heart of the church community.[20] They move from being a service user to becoming a service provider. They start referring to the church as 'their' church, not 'your' church or 'that' church. They now have a greater sense of ownership through service.

Change your mind

Service is never about getting a job done; that is the end result, not the purpose. Service changes the heart and shows a different way of living. That's why Jesus washed His disciples' feet to set an example to them:

> You call me 'Teacher' and 'Lord,' and you are right, because
> that's what I am. And since I, your Lord and Teacher,
> have washed your feet, you ought to wash each other's
> feet. I have given you an example to follow. Do as I have
> done to you.
> John 13:13–15

Service changes our mindset. Rather than thinking, 'What can I get out of this?', it makes us realise we have something to offer. Service stops us from becoming self-centered and self-absorbed with our problems. Service helps us realise that everyone is facing some kind of challenge, and gives a new perspective on our own issues.

I'd love to challenge you here: ring up your vicar, church leader, pastor or minister and offer to serve in any way that you can (go on, it will freak them out a little!). Get on a team, get sucked into the 'rotas', serve others by imitating Jesus. It won't just be helpful – it will change you. Don't just attend and observe church. Get involved and get connected to those that sit next to you on a Sunday or who look a little awkward with their cup of tea in the corner, because people *really* matter. That's the way Jesus operated with His small group of disciples and the way He had time for the crowds that followed Him.

The purpose of the Church is not to become cool and culturally relevant, but to create an authentic culture that then naturally becomes attractive and inviting because people want to belong, and because they have an inbuilt desire to be connected to others and to the God who created them. And as we fulfil Jesus' last prayer in John 17 to become more united, more people will be drawn to the church family because of how we reflect God and the love He has for the world:

> make me truly happy by agreeing wholeheartedly with
> each other, loving one another, and working together with
> one mind and purpose.
> Philippians 2:2

I genuinely believe, naively perhaps, that the rest will work itself out in our churches if we simply love one another and work together with one mind and purpose.

Become a gatherer

We need to look out for ways to help new visitors in our churches feel at home, to get there early and seek out those who seem disconnected in the church meeting or haven't made those connections yet. Help someone feel at home; invite them to your small group; find out what gifts they have; introduce them to other people with similar interests; remember their name and look out for them; invite them to sit next to you. The simplest actions could have lifelong implications.

Grow

No one is
finished yet

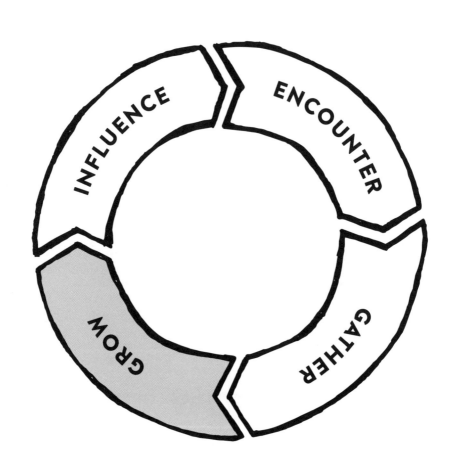

Grow fruitfully

> It's not important who does the planting, or who does
> the watering. What's important is that God makes
> the seed grow.
> 1 Corinthians 3:7

I know very little about gardening. I know that if I don't mow the lawn, the grass gets longer, and if I don't pull up the weeds, they take over the flowerbeds... that's about it. Fortunately, my dad loves gardening and sees it as his personal responsibility to come over to my home from time to time and ensure the garden is under control.

Every living thing grows, but not everything grows strong. Planting seeds isn't enough – you have to nurture them in a safe environment until they are strong enough to be transplanted from their safe little pot to the dangerous outside world. The same is true of people who come to faith. As a church community it is our responsibility to help people grow in their understanding, to keep them safe while they are getting to grips with the basics of Christianity, but they can't stay in the safe, warm, dry spiritual greenhouse forever. Eventually they need some real-world exposure so they can put their new-found faith into action.

It's also true that plants can get stuck in their growth. They get crowded by other plants, or damaged by the weather, or the ground is no longer giving them the nutrients they need. People who have been Christians for a bit longer can easily get a bit stunted in their growth. They feel overcrowded by the busyness of life, negatively affected by the environment in which they find themselves, or perhaps the church they are part of is no longer giving them the challenge that they need to keep growing.

If a church doesn't develop its growth strategy, then it will start sending ill-prepared seedlings into a challenging environment or it will have ageing plants that are creating little or no fruit.

Just as you can tell a lot about a tree by looking at its fruit, you can tell a lot about a person by their character. Godly character cannot be forced or faked – it is evidence of the Holy Spirit working in us.

Jesus said:

> A tree is identified by its fruit... A good person produces good things from the treasury of a good heart, and an evil person produces evil things from the treasury of an evil heart. What you say flows from what is in your heart.
> Luke 6:44–45

How fruitful are our lives? How fruitful are our churches? Are we rooted in Christ? We need to regularly examine the fruit we are growing as it will show evidence of where our roots are truly planted. The Fruit of the Spirit that we should be producing is listed in Galatians as: love, joy, peace, patience, kindness, goodness, faithfulness, gentleness and self-control (Gal. 5:22). It is the external evidence of internal growth. If our churches are full of unloving, miserable, irate, impatient, unkind, bad, unfaithful, harsh and out-of-control people, then we should run a mile and find a new church.

Our external behaviour flows from what is in our hearts, and how we treat someone will always reflect what is going on inside.

Seeds carry potential

When we choose to follow Jesus and are filled with His Holy Spirit, He does not choose to make us loving, joyful and peaceful overnight, but we have within us the potential to become all of those things. The Fruit of the Spirit is like a row of nine seeds that have been planted into our lives on the day we choose to follow Jesus:

> By his divine power, God has given us everything we need
> for living a godly life.
> 2 Peter 1:3

Seeds of potential are not enough on their own. We still need the Holy Spirit to help us bear good fruit. It's a bit like how an apple contains the potential for an entire orchard – but if I was to throw a soggy apple core out of the car window while driving down a country lane, I wouldn't then expect to see apple trees shooting up at the side of the road on my return journey. It would need a much more controlled environment. To grow an apple tree you have to take the seed out of the apple, cleanse it, plant it in a pot, ensure it is kept at the right temperature, water it regularly, not give it too much sun... and when the plant starts to sprout, you then need to repot it. When it is much stronger, take it outside to repot it again, and after a year, place it in the ground – ensuring it is in good soil, gets the right amount of sun and is watered regularly. A carefully maintained apple tree in a controlled environment will take around six to ten years to produce its first crop of fruit.

It takes time to grow as a Christian too – to develop healthy disciplines and to nurture who we are becoming.

Grow through self-control

I reckon the most frequently overlooked Fruit of the Spirit is the last one on the list: self-control. I have spent years in church meetings and conferences all round the world, singing hundreds of worship songs about love, joy, peace... but I don't ever remember singing one about self-control. I'm not sure that that song has even been written, and yet it is such an important Fruit of the Spirit. We don't seem to want to talk about it, and yet it is probably the one that will help us grow the most.

Self-control is the forgotten Fruit. It is the one that nobody likes to discuss. Maybe it's because all of us struggle in this area in some way, which stops us from growing as a follower of Christ – and yet, self-control represents an important attribute of a disciple: discipline! Self-control is listed with all these other things we can agree are very *good*. And the fact that it's on the list means we need the Spirit's help with it.

It could be argued that a lack of self-control is the reason why so much goes wrong in our world. Self-obsession is often at the root of our poor decision making: our foolish moments of sexual immorality, drunken behaviour or well-hidden addictions. A lack of self-control has been to blame for many a volcanic eruption on social media. It always amazes me how often people say things online that they would never say in front of their work colleagues, friends or family. People have lost jobs, lost trust in a relationship, lost respect – all because of one impulsive, digital response.

We live in a selfie culture, where self comes first. We are not controlling ourselves; we are allowing 'self' to be in control. We will never grow stronger while telling ourselves that whatever we want, we can have. When our selfish desires are out of control, we become egotistical and self-absorbed. So, though it may come 'last' in the list, I am increasingly convinced that we need self-control in tandem with the Holy Spirit to develop the seeds of love, joy, peace, patience, kindness, goodness, faithfulness and gentleness into real tangible Fruit, so that we can be 'mature and complete, not lacking anything' (James 1:4, NIV).

True growth comes when self is challenged, shaped and restrained in some way. Yet something I've noticed is that when church leaders have their regular meetings, they may discuss church business, caring for people and the vision of the church, they may talk about doing good, loving our neighbour, maybe even gentleness to those who are facing difficulties, but rarely do leaders challenge each other on self-control. Why is this the case, when New Testament writings on leadership seem to value it so highly?

> So a church leader must be a man whose life is above reproach. He must be faithful to his wife. He must exercise *self-control*, live wisely, and have a good reputation. He must enjoy having guests in his home, and he must be able to teach.
>
> 1 Timothy 3:2 (emphasis added)

When I am having a pastoral conversation with someone who has upset someone else or caused disagreement, we might talk about being kind, becoming more loving, making peace – but never self-control. And yet the apostle Peter didn't shy away from this at all:

> Supplement your faith with a generous provision of moral
> excellence, and moral excellence with knowledge, and
> knowledge with *self-control*, and *self-control* with patient
> endurance, and patient endurance with godliness, and
> godliness with brotherly affection, and brotherly affection
> with love for everyone.
>
> 2 Peter 1:5–7 (emphasis added)

I want the Church to be courageous: full of well-rooted, self-controlled disciples who always think of others before themselves: people who, before reacting with shock or horror at the behaviour of the world around us or even another church in our community, pause for a moment before we respond with some self-control. When we do this, we are growing as followers of Christ.

When it comes to personal growth as a disciple of Jesus, you can have control over your faithfulness, but very little over your fruitfulness, as that is dependent on the Holy Spirit choosing to work through you. But I am convinced that as we take control of ourselves, the Holy Spirit will be more inclined to create opportunities where we can become fruitful. We alone are responsible for our actions. Self-control is where we begin to grow.

I have heard it said many times that 'people grow through experience', but I don't believe that's true.

I have met a huge number of 'experienced' people who aren't growing – they are just having one experience after another. No one is challenging their decisions, no one is coming alongside them offering support, no one is celebrating their successes, and they have no plan of how to grow. They might have a desire to grow, but there is a big difference between having a goal and having a step-by-step strategy to reach that goal. People grow through *assessed* experience, through planning the way they want to grow.

Planning for growth

> Those who are *planted in the house* of the LORD
> Shall flourish in the courts of our God.
> They shall still bear fruit in old age;
> They shall be fresh and flourishing
> Psalm 92:13–14 (NKJV, emphasis added)

People who are 'planted in the house of the Lord' (fully participating in the life of a healthy church), will see growth in all aspects of their life. But this growth does not happen accidentally – it requires a deliberate plan. A school does not invite students to attend each day to decide what they might want to learn. There is a curriculum, designed to help pupils grow in their education. They have a plan. A personal trainer does not invite their clients to simply run around the gym and try whatever machine looks interesting: once they have discovered what the person they are helping is trying to achieve, they will create a plan. Serious gardeners don't just throw a bag of seeds onto the ground and hope for the best. They have a plan. They work out the best time of year, the right soil, the right environmental factors, and then plant carefully, followed by regular checkups and watering. They have a plan. So why is it that when it comes to growing in their Christian faith, many people attend church sporadically, dip into the Bible occasionally, and pray impatiently when they have an emergency?

As a sidebar here, I think it's worth touching on growth through suffering. When you look back at your life, I am certain that the seasons in which you have grown the most will often have been the most difficult times of your life. One of the most common questions we get asked when we run Alpha is, 'Why is there suffering in the world?', yet the Bible often encourages us to celebrate times of trial and frustration. When the apostle Peter was writing his letters around AD 65, it was during a time of fierce Christian persecution, with those following 'the way' being set alight like candles by wealthy hosts for the entertainment of their guests, or being thrown to packs of wild animals in sporting arenas for the enjoyment of those watching. In the middle of such extreme opposition, which presumably dwarfs most of our modern-day experiences of 'religious persecution', Peter wrote these words:

> So be truly glad. There is wonderful joy ahead, even though you must endure many trials for a little while. These trials will show that your faith is genuine. It is being tested as fire tests and purifies gold—though your faith is far more precious than mere gold. So when your faith remains strong through many trials, it will bring you much praise and glory and honor on the day when Jesus Christ is revealed to the whole world.
>
> 1 Peter 1:6–7

So, rather than feel frustrated by the disappointments that come your way, see them as opportunities to grow, to welcome the difficulties and lean into God, our rock and place of safety (Psa. 18:2).

Back to that plan, then. What is your plan for personal growth? What is your church's plan to see regular attenders become fully mature followers of Christ?

At Freedom Church, we try to think in terms of 'steps' rather than 'programmes', and structure our growth plan with a series of courses that people can attend to learn about particular aspects of the Christian faith: the culture of our church, how to listen to God, getting free from past issues, what God might be calling you into, etc. They work on a term-time basis and run within small groups (which people sign up to). These are helpful, but attending a series of courses doesn't guarantee growth. There is the risk that all we are doing with such activities is creating a list that people feel obliged to complete: a 'smorgasbord' of programmes.[21] The timetables we come up with might look beautiful on paper, but the Church is not an educational establishment creating curriculums for people to complete and get the certificate for. We might become professors of theology who can recite every red-letter word of Jesus, but if we are not loving to those around us, then have we truly grown in our faith or just become more knowledgeable? I really believe that the purpose of the Church is not to create clever attendees, but to create a movement of broken people learning to live more like Jesus every day. People really matter, and the real growth happens in our interaction with one another. I love this quote from David Tripp:

> The church is not a theological classroom. It is a conversion, confession, repentance, reconciliation, forgiveness and sanctification center, where flawed people place their faith in Christ, gather to know and love him better, and learn to love others as he designed.[22]

Equally, before you start googling the latest discipleship programme, I just want to point out that any change that you want to make starts with you (and we're back to self-control again!). The dietician may give you an excellent diet plan, but if you stuff your face with whatever you like when they're not looking, the plan won't make any difference. The conductor may be following a beautiful musical score, but if you prefer to tootle along with your own tune (or just pretend to play the right notes, which is what I did in my junior school's recorder performance of *London's Burning*), the score goes out the window.

A number of years ago I had the opportunity to run the London Marathon for Links International, a charity that I was a trustee of, and a member of my church who was a personal trainer offered to help me prepare. Each session he would push me to run harder, faster, to lift more, stretch further... It was exhausting being forced to do something that I naturally wanted to stop doing. I remember on one occasion, while gasping for air, asking my overenthusiastic (in my opinion) personal trainer whether I really needed to do all this work. Could we not slow it down a little, lift a little less, run a little slower? I will never forget his response: 'Of course you can, but you will only be cheating yourself.' In the same way, if we *say* we are a follower of Jesus – with all the outward activity that we think is supposed to go with it – but never practise becoming more like Him, we are only cheating ourselves.

Spiritual growth comes through spending time with God and His people. It's as simple as that. However good the discipleship programme we have picked out of the internet 'hat' might be, time with God and time with other disciples is essential – there is no magic podcast or daily Bible reading notes that will do all the work for you. This might sound like a lot of effort, but I promise it is worth it. It takes more than one ten-minute walk on a treadmill to prepare for a marathon, but the training plan needn't be complicated.

I know there are some out there that might believe the traditional 'quiet time' is old-fashioned and unnecessary. The idea of kneeling by the bed (or quietly sitting in a cosy armchair reading a large leather-bound Bible by the fire) creates images of yesteryear, not the modern society of today. We have so much to do and fit into our day that the idea of stopping and pausing seems ridiculous – and yet this is what Jesus did. He regularly took Himself away and spent time with His Father. It is far more important to copy the ways of Jesus than to imitate the world and always be squeezing a little more into our day, constantly rushing to the next appointment.

If having time with God has never been part of your daily routine, here are some simple steps to get you started.

Create a habit

Good habits are actually quite freeing – they mean we accomplish good things almost on autopilot. One study from Duke University found that more than 40% of the actions people take every day aren't conscious decisions, but habits.[23] Find a regular time and space – whether that is early morning before the kids get up, mid-morning over a coffee when there is a lull in the office, or maybe the evening before bed. Go with whatever works for you. We are all made differently. I'm a morning person and love the early hours. I have a favourite chair in my study, and that's where I sit and begin my day. It doesn't matter if you do it on the commute to work, going for a walk with the dog or lying in bed – there are no rules, just find a time and make an appointment. Seriously, make it an appointment. Put it in your diary or your smartphone or write it on a daily to-do list, but book it in. It might feel a little strange at first, but in time it will become part of a daily habit.

Start small

Don't try to spend an hour a day on your knees in prayer and two hours reading the Bible. Start small. Life changes always begin with small adjustments. One model, suggested by Cris Rogers in his book *Making Disciples*,[24] suggests you start with six minutes: three minutes reading a couple of Bible verses, two minutes praying and one minute in quiet. He has worked out that this can all be achieved in the time it takes to boil a kettle and make a cup of tea.

Whatever you choose to do in your time with God, start small. He would rather have your full attention for a small amount of time than none of your time. Even if it is just a moment in your day where you stop, consider Jesus and give your day to Him, then that's a good start.

What do you do?

If you're the sort of person who finds it helpful to have a bit of structure, here's a suggestion for what you might like to include in your time with God each day.

Pause. Stop for a moment before rushing in and blurting out all your problems to God. Pause, be quiet and listen. Just enjoy being alone with God for a moment.

Read. I still believe the Bible is the inspired Word of God, and although it is thousands of years old and written by a number of human authors, it has something to say to each one of us today. I make it a habit to read a portion of the Bible each day using a Bible reading app so that I read it all the way through each year. I would encourage the habit of reading the Bible each day, even if only a few verses to start with.

Pray. This is not just a list of requests, but a conversation with God. Start with prayers of thanks – find something to be grateful for before bringing the needs of those you love and the challenges you may be facing. Speak to God about the day ahead or behind, but also wait and listen – see what He has to say.

Ponder. Don't just rush away. Consider what you have heard, read and experienced. This is my big challenge. Practise the art of sitting still.

Apply. It doesn't have to be a radical life-changing decision, but put something into action. It might simply be to call a friend or family member and encourage them. Take something you have been praying about and make it part of your day. Small actions are always better than inaction.

When it comes to making time spent with God a regular thing, simply keep going. Some days the Word of God will come alive, and other days it might seem pretty empty, but *keep going*. Make a daily appointment with God, knowing that this habit will create growth in you and opportunities to encounter God afresh. When we stop giving God our attention, something changes in us that will be first noticed by those closest to us. We don't want to become legalistic, but we do want to create life-giving habits. We are always with God if we are following Him. He has promised to always be with us and never forsake us. You can talk with God at any time during the day. The conversation doesn't need to end when you say 'Amen'.

If we want our churches, families and friends to be growing in their faith and being stretched in their understanding of God, it starts with you and me. Divert daily and see what God will do in those few moments with Him.

Grow through others

To grow in our faith, we need to spend time with others who are trying to do the same. Discipleship never happens in isolation.

> As iron sharpens iron,
> so a friend sharpens a friend.
> Proverbs 27:17

You're far more likely to get in the gym if you're meeting a friend for a workout. Just like having a running partner, mutual accountability between Christians is a game-changer. Find yourself a 'piece of iron' who can encourage you when you are not at your best, and offer their support when you are struggling. Your honesty and vulnerability will pay dividends.

When I eventually ran the London Marathon, I ran with my brother Mark. We had trained separately as we live a distance apart, but we agreed that we would run together. Following the advice of some experienced marathon runners, I wrote my name on the front of my shirt so the crowd could cheer me on by name. Throughout the whole course, people shouted personal encouragement to me to keep going. It was so powerful. But there came a moment around mile 21 when both my legs cramped up. I was in trouble, and the crowd shouting my name was not going to help me at this point. Mark, who had probably trained harder than me (story of our lives), stayed with me. Fortunately, the race organisers prepare for this sort of thing and we found a physio at the side of the road – and after receiving some pretty intense massage, I found my second wind. A couple more miles later, as we were heading to the last part of the course, it was my brother's turn to struggle and my turn to encourage him. After more than 26 miles running side by side, we crossed the finish line at exactly the same moment, and I knew that I would not have completed the race without him. The writer of the book of Hebrews described the Christian life like this:

> And let us run with endurance the race God has set before us. We do this by fixing our eyes on Jesus, the champion who initiates and perfects our faith.
> Hebrews 12:1

So yes, we need to keep our eyes fixed on Jesus. But we also need each other to help us up when we fall down. This is discipleship: walking in the footsteps of Jesus with others around us: friends, companions and fellow disciples.

If we want to grow as followers of Jesus, we need to actively look for others to grow alongside. In *No Perfect People Allowed*,[25] John Burke talks about a system of 'running partners', where people are encouraged to pair up with someone for mutual accountability. For me personally, this is preferable to the concept of mentoring, where there is always an expert, the 'seasoned follower', who is supporting the apprentice disciple, the new member of the class. One teaches the other based on their greater knowledge and experience (which sounds to me more like the relationship between Mr Miyagi and the Karate Kid). The point is that the Christian faith is not full of experts and beginners, gurus and newbies. We are called to run this race like Jesus did and point others to Him. Of course, it's vital we learn from more experienced Christians and honour those who have consistently lived the 'long walk of obedience in the same direction',[26] but we are called to imitate Christ (Eph. 5:1), not our church leader.

I used to meet up weekly with one of my young leaders to provide mentorship. At first, I was the experienced leader offering advice to the younger leader, but after a number of months I realised I was gaining as much out of the experience as he (hopefully) was. We were both growing, but learning different things. We can learn so much from one another, however experienced we might be. People are remarkable and contain the very essence of their creator God, but some require more patience to discover the gold within. It is always there if we are willing to spend the time.

If you want to set up a 'running partnership', here are a few thoughts to get started.

1. Find a buddy. Find someone you like being with (if they annoy you, it's not going to last), but do find someone who is different to you – someone at a different stage of life, older or younger than you – doesn't really matter. It should ideally be with someone of the same sex for a number of reasons – largely so that you'll be able to talk about certain subjects without it being inappropriate. You may also be able to be more real with them. What's most important is that you share the same desire to grow. When the Bible talks about being unequally yoked (2 Cor. 6:14, NKJV), it's not necessarily talking solely about nice Christian teenage girls going out with those naughty non-Christian boys. It's warning us to be walking with people who have a similar level of passion for the things of God. If you

partner up with someone who just wants a coffee and doesn't want to change, then it will start to frustrate you.

2. Agree a purpose. When you first meet up, agree what part of your Christian faith you would like to grow in. You will have different goals, and that's OK. You are not competing with each other but supporting each other to achieve your personal goals. Ensure that each goal is clear, and write it down somewhere so you can refer back to it in the future (maybe in a notebook, not on the back of a napkin that you will never see again after you chuck it in the bin by mistake).

3. Decide on a time frame. There's no set rule for this: I tend to operate on a school year from September to July, which works well for students and those with school-age children, but may not work so well for everyone. It may just be for a month or for a year. Obviously, you can always revisit this after you've been meeting for a while.

4. Meet up regularly. This might sound obvious, but create a habit of meeting up regularly, whether weekly or monthly, and do what you can to stick to it. Find a time and a place that works for both of you, where you can be fully focused on the other's needs. Set a limit on the length of your meeting so that you make it more efficient. You can do this in a lunch hour, or even 30 minutes if you are really focused. It's easy for a whole morning to disappear while you meander around various subjects rather than jumping straight in and talking about what's really important to you.

5. Communicate. With the technology we have today, it's easy (and helpful) to stay in touch between meetings. If concerns are coming to mind or you're facing a challenge, you can message your running partner and ask them to pray or give you some advice. A quick message is always better than

struggling with a particular issue and then sharing your concerns weeks later at your next meeting.

6. Have a plan. You could follow a particular book about a key subject that you want to grow in, follow Bible notes together, listen to the same podcast or unpack what you've learnt from your church's Sunday teaching. In a recent discipleship group for men that I have been running, we had a programme of ten core topics that we covered each month with a challenge to complete before the next time we met. Just have a plan. Frustration appears when there is a difference between what each person expects and the reality of what they experience.

7. Be accountable. Be honest and vulnerable with each other. You don't have share everything, but if you keep your guard up and hold back, then your running partner will mirror that behaviour. If you are the 'more experienced' Christian in your partnership, then you need to take responsibility by going first. Then hold each other to account. If you said you wanted to make a change, don't be surprised if the other person asks you how that change is going. Vulnerability takes courage, but it is how we grow.

8. Keep assessing. Is it working? Are you both growing? Keep going back to your original target and see if you are more on-track than when you started. The aim is always mutual growth. If it's not working, you may want to rewrite your plan or find a new running partner. This may be challenging to your relationship, but if neither of you are growing through the experience then it might be better to find new partners.

Meeting up with someone and learning together can be exciting and invigorating, but that's not the ultimate aim. Growth is. Becoming more like Jesus and living your life the way He would want you to.

Becoming a better parent, spouse, child, employee, employer, leader, follower or team player.

Pastoral care

OK, so let me confess here: this is my weakness. I have been accused by some of not being very pastoral. I do like people – honest. I think people are amazing. But when people become 'needy' and they want you to fix them, I can get a little frustrated. I know many people won't understand this, but it is no secret to my family or my church team, and I'm working on it – honest.

I want people in our churches to flourish; I want them to grow healthy and be amazing, but there is sometimes a strange psychology that happens around churches where people in need see the Church simply as a rescue centre to permanently help them out. Sometimes the Church can give the perception that we are nice people, who like helping people. We run food banks and debt counselling and street pastoring and after-school clubs and homeless shelters… we are kind. But I believe these relationships can become unhealthy if people are always taking and never contributing. (By the way, my wife won't agree with any of this and will probably try to edit it out of the book – she is much more pastoral than I am and wants to help everyone she sees who is in need.) We are called to help others, but I think there is a better model than simply running around trying to fix everyone who is asking for help. I was in the fire service for a number of years and we were trained, in an emergency situation such as a car crash or a house fire, to give priority to those who are silent rather than those who are most vocal. I find it fascinating that in a church you can have people complaining at great volume about every minor challenge they are facing, while others will be struggling with a life-threatening illness and not tell a soul. How do we really help each other to grow stronger, and not just create unhealthy, dependent relationships between those who love to help and those who love to receive help?

The Bible often uses the analogy of Jesus as a good shepherd – perhaps most notably in the parable of the lost sheep (see Matt. 18:12–14 or Luke 15:3–7). The role of the shepherd was to provide safety and nourishment. Sometimes one would go off-track and need rescuing, but sheep tend to stick together (as they know that if they do, they will be provided with clean water, plenty of grass and safety from anything that would wish them harm).I find it fascinating that we have turned that model around from 99 sheep being provided for and staying together while the shepherd goes to look for the one, to there now seemingly being only one sheep left in the pen while the shepherd runs around the countryside trying to persuade the 99 that they will be safe and well-watered if they could possibly come back to church next Sunday.

The church leader is not there to provide for each and every member's personal needs, but to provide a safe place and good nourishment (Acts 20:28). Fortunately for our church family, we have a wonderful team that co-ordinates pastoral care across the church. Meals are regularly provided, visits are arranged, flowers are delivered and people are cared for. I am so glad (and so is my church) that I am not on my own in sorting all this out. It just wouldn't happen. As it goes, I am very grateful for the different gifts that other people bring.

When we look at the Early Church in the book of Acts, we see that they shared everything they had with those in need. It was never meant to be the few looking after the many, but the community looking after each other. The Church should be a loving caring community, where each person is looking out for others.

In Acts 6, we see that the apostles appointed seven men to co-ordinate the care of the widows and the orphans – to help shape the culture of care, not necessarily the care itself. These seven were administrators of high standing and wisdom, who would free up the apostles for prayer and preaching. The Early Church appointed co-ordinators, not pastors – people held in high esteem amongst their peers.

Can the words 'pastoral' and 'strategy' ever go together?

In churches, we tend to place people who are pastorally minded in charge of our pastoral teams. But sometimes people who love caring for others are not the right people to have in charge of developing a strategy of care. I have noticed that if you get enough pastoral people in a room, they will start praying for those on the team and offering support to each other. I know this is a generalisation, but often those who are people-minded are not the same as those who are systems-focused. If we want to care for those in need in our church community and beyond, then we need both.

I remember reading about an army doctor who was sent to a warzone to care for the injured. They jumped out of the helicopter and got straight to work. When they came to the first person in need, they stopped and administered first aid – then the next person, then the next. On and on they worked. Every patient that was presented to them became the next emergency. The patients loved their doctor, who was available to them any time of day or night. But after a couple of weeks of working this way, the doctor collapsed in exhaustion and had to be airlifted back to base for some respite, taking them months to fully recover. The replacement doctor arrived. This one was a little different. They assessed the warzone and compiled a list of casualties and main injuries. They recognised the need, but also realised that they would need support. This new doctor radioed back to base and said that they would be unable to start work until they had more medical equipment, suitable medication and a team with specific skills who could work together to create a healthy and sustainable field hospital that would provide quality care for those that were facing the greatest injuries.[27]

We need a strategy when it comes to caring for others. It's not that I don't care about people – it's the exact opposite. I care enough that I want to do it well. I really do believe that the Church should be the best at caring for those who are struggling and helping them flourish. To do that will require careful planning, not just well-meaning people burning themselves out in their desire to help those in need around them.

There's a few things we've tried at Freedom Church that we've found to be really helpful in terms of strategising our care. First, we encourage initial care to take place in our connect groups. If people in the groups have concerns or challenges that they are facing, then they should communicate it to the rest of the group in an appropriate manner and ask for support.

We also have a practical support team. People in our church have signed up to say that they have certain skills that they would love to use to help others who are unable to help themselves. On the list we have people who are good at gardening, basic DIY, sewing, driving, babysitting, filling in forms, etc. We also have a vast team of people that love to cook. If you move to a new house, have a baby or are dealing with a bereavement, then you will be provided with hot meals for you and your family. It is amazing how many people love to help others in this way, especially when it seems like there is little you can do to help practically.

Behind the care that happens in the groups and teams I've just mentioned is our pastoral care team, which co-ordinates all the care that happens across the church. They are the first to know when there is a need, will delegate the care to the right people, make suitable notes for future awareness and ensure that there is ongoing support for the individual. The team also work with other agencies such as health services, social services and mental health provision to ensure that we co-ordinate care for those requiring specialist support. Ultimately, we don't want our churches to have a highly organised care programme just for the sake of it: we want to replicate the authenticity of the Early Church and its culture of care, encouraging people to look out for those in need and not to wait for permission to provide a meal, send some flowers, write a card or pop round for a cup of tea.

The best way of providing pastoral care in a church is to encourage health in the community, and that's health in all areas – physically, mentally and spiritually. Be pro-active in providing care rather than reactive when it all goes wrong. We know it is better to maintain and service our cars regularly or attend the dentist for checkups to keep our teeth healthy, but still many people wait until the car breaks down or the tooth needs a filling before seeking help. It is often the same in the area of pastoral care in our churches. People ask for help in their damaged relationships, ongoing addictions and personal frustrations when something has broken and the church has become a last-ditch attempt at saving things. If only those same people knew they could ask for help when they had their first marital spat, the first time they took drugs, the first time they stayed up late to watch pornography or the first time they struggled with feeling like a failure in their workplace.

The most caring thing we can do as a church is love people by pointing them back to Jesus, who by His death on the cross took all our sin, pain and suffering and gave us life in all its fullness. Jesus did not die so we could moan about how unfair life is. He took our place so that we could have full access to His Father. This is what He came to do:

> The Spirit of the Sovereign Lord is on me,
>   because the Lord has anointed me
>   to proclaim good news to the poor.
> He has sent me to bind up the broken-hearted,
>   to proclaim freedom for the captives
>   and release from darkness for the prisoners,
> to proclaim the year of the LORD's favour
>   and the day of vengeance of our God,
> to comfort all who mourn,
>   and provide for those who grieve in Zion –
> to bestow on them a crown of beauty
>   instead of ashes,
> the oil of joy
>   instead of mourning,
> and a garment of praise
>   instead of a spirit of despair.
> They will be called oaks of righteousness,
>   a planting of the LORD
>   for the display of his splendour.
> Isaiah 61:1–3 (NIV)

This is our mission statement too. Our responsibility as the local church is to reflect God here on earth: to comfort those who mourn, bind up the broken-hearted and release the prisoners from darkness. But oaks of righteousness don't become established overnight. It may take years of planting, nurturing and support before the people in our churches are called the 'display of his splendour' – but what a title to receive!

I think it's really important to mention that there is also a personal responsibility for pastoral care – to ask for help when in need, not just assume that people will know you need help:

> Are any of you sick? You should call for the elders of the
> church to come and pray over you, anointing you with oil in
> the name of the Lord.
> James 5:14

If you are part of a church and you need help, please ask. Sometimes people assume that if the church really cared, they would just *know* that they need help – so they never ask for it. When no help comes, they label the church as uncaring and head off to the next one in the town. At that point, everyone has lost out: the person in need, the ones that would have loved to provide care and the reputation of the church. We can do better, but each one of us needs to take responsibility.

Finally, pastoral care should never be the main focus of the local church. We are a mission organisation with a great commission to fulfil. In the famous quote attributed to Abigail Van Buren, who created the 'Dear Abby' column in the mid-twentieth century, 'The church is a hospital for sinners, not a museum for saints.' Or, as Jesus put it (and I personally like this a bit better):

> Healthy people don't need a doctor—sick people do. I have
> come to call not those who think they are righteous, but
> those who know they are sinners.
> Mark 2:17

The Church isn't about us and our needs. It is always about others. Others who are broken-hearted, bound up and lost. We are called to serve others. It is *always* about others. If each member of the church body focused on helping the others, all would receive care and support – and, after all, is it not better to give than to receive?

Grow through the Holy Spirit

Ultimately, we want people in our churches to grow. Not through our ability to care for each other or through our teaching programmes, but directly from God Himself. If we want to grow to become more like Jesus, then we need to be looking to Him, not our fallible, human-led churches.

When Jesus left earth, He gave some advice to His disciples who were with Him as He ascended (that must have been a moment that they would never forget!):

> But you will receive power when the Holy Spirit comes
> upon you. And you will be my witnesses, telling people
> about me everywhere—in Jerusalem, throughout Judea, in
> Samaria, and to the ends of the earth.
> Acts 1:8

If we are going to be effective in our fourth 'quadrant' and be an influence in our world (more on that coming up), then we need the Holy Spirit. There is a clear connection between needing the power of the Holy Spirit and the completion of the great commission by going into all the world and preaching the gospel. We cannot do it in our own strength: we need the courage, power and comfort that the Holy Spirit gives us.

In his book *The Promise of the Holy Spirit*,[28] my brother-in-law, Rich Hubbard, used the analogy of the Holy Spirit as being like a set of tools in a toolbox – there to be activated and used, not just left to get rusty and dusty. We seem happy enough to talk about the Fruit of the Spirit, yet in so many of our churches today, the *gifts* of the Spirit conjure up distant memories of charismatic craziness with flag waving, singing in tongues and banging sticks (yes, that was a thing) – which might cause some of the 'tidier' churches of today a level of discomfort. In 1 Corinthians 12, Paul lists a variety of gifts given to us by the Holy Spirit for each one of us to *use*. They are different gifts, but the same Spirit – but still we want to pick and choose. We want the Fruit of the Spirit in our churches, but when it comes to the gifts of the same Spirit, we are a little more hesitant. I can feel it in myself. The potential for messiness increases. 'We just got it all so tidy and now we are going to invite the Holy Spirit in.'

But this tension makes no sense. It is the same Spirit. Some churches aspire to prophesy, speak in tongues, have words of knowledge but pay lip service to kindness and gentleness. At the same time, other churches talk loudly about love and joy but see the gifts of the Spirit as no longer necessary for today's Church. But I would argue the gifts cannot be separated from the fruit – they come from the same source. The Holy Spirit is not there to bring mayhem or disorder but to help, give wise advice, special knowledge, faith, healing, miracles, prophecy, discernment, to speak in different languages and to interpret those languages (1 Cor. 12:7–10). He is a gift to each one of us, and a real gift to the Church. If the Holy Spirit really is allowed to flow through all that we do, then that means we can't separate Him into the parts we like and are comfortable with, with the rest consigned to the bottom drawer of our church activities.

Paul recognises that we won't all have every gift, but says we are to 'earnestly desire' them (1 Cor. 12:31). Then, a little later on in his first letter to the Corinthians, he says:

> Let love be your highest goal! But you should also desire the special abilities the Spirit gives
> 1 Corinthians 14:1

The chapter that comes in between these instructions concerning spiritual gifts is the famous 1 Corinthians 13, which talks all about love. Yes, love is the 'greatest of these' (1 Cor. 13:13), but while we should pursue it, let's not settle *only* for love. Paul is saying to the church in Corinth to eagerly desire it all – the Fruit *and* the gifts – but don't pursue the gifts without putting down a foundation of love first.

Leaning in

Paul encourages us to live by the Spirit as a normal part of our everyday lives (Gal. 5:5). I know that when I am living in step with the Spirit, I am in the best place. I am growing stronger because I am reliant on God and not on my own strength. As Christians, we don't grow only through attending church, listening to sermons, going to conferences or reading books: we grow in our faith when we start to *lean in* to the Holy Spirit through times of uncertainty.

Spiritual growth is not about more knowledge in our heads, more love in our hearts or more service to our community. As good as those things might be, spiritual growth is about waking up each day and walking in step with the Holy Spirit. It's letting Him lead us, even though we may go through some of the darkest places, and letting Him provide us with the best nourishment, that we might grow.

What about our church services on a Sunday, then? Should we just turn up with no plan and see what the Spirit might do? If we're not careful, there is a fine line between leaning into the Holy Spirit, and simply being a little bit lazy in our preparations. I believe we should be organised, but remain open – leaving space for the Spirit to work how and when He wants to. God told Noah to build the ark years before there was a drop of rain (Gen. 6). Jesus talked to His disciples about counting the cost of a project and planning it well (Luke 14:28). Plans are important. Even if it's a simple one scribbled on the back of an envelope, have a plan and then see what God will do with willing servants who are comfortable responding to the nudging of His Spirit. But remember that our plans are always the servant, never the master. Our plans must never become idols we worship.

A church without the Holy Spirit and the gifts He offers makes little sense. He is vital to our gatherings and essential to our growth. When writing to the Corinthian church, Paul instructed the believers to use their spiritual gifts to build one another up:

> When you meet together, one will sing, another will teach, another will tell some special revelation God has given, one will speak in tongues, and another will interpret what is said. But everything that is done must strengthen all of you.
> 1 Corinthians 14:26

It's worth asking ourselves, if we are not using our spiritual gifts to build others up, can we really call ourselves an authentic church?

I love the analogy that Dave Smith (Senior Pastor of Kingsgate Church) uses. He likens the Holy Spirit to a swimming pool with a shallow end and a deep end. He suggests that our Sunday services should be at the shallow end, where newcomers and guests can paddle in the Holy Spirit, getting used to the water in a safe environment – but you also need a deep end, where people can experience the Holy Spirit in full depth, getting soaked in His presence, drenched in His power and prepared for what is ahead.

Influence

Every person
can create change

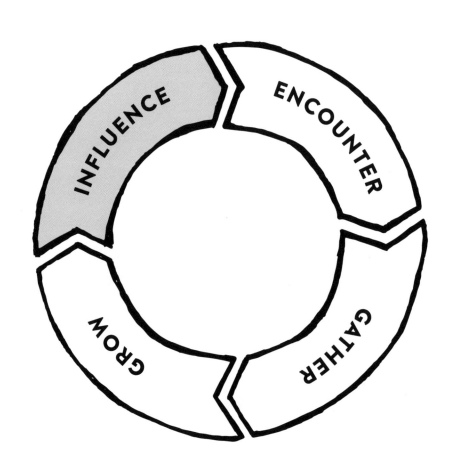

Influence always starts with people

In Genesis, we read that when God made the heavens and the earth, He looked at what He had created and saw that it was good (Gen. 1:31). Human beings are incredible: we are made in the image of God, and when we put our minds to work, share our ideas and turn our dreams into a reality by working with others, it is amazing what can be achieved. From farming to moon landings, from hunting to splitting atoms, from basic survival to curing diseases, from rudimentary tools to advanced technology – the list of mankind's achievements, positive or otherwise, is endless.

People achieve the impossible when their God-given gift influences others. Our unique talents are never meant to be a secret power that we keep to ourselves. Influence is taking what we have and making it a gift to others for the improvement of the world that we share.

Jesus said He would build His Church (Matt. 16:18) – a community full of His people. We are supposed to be impactful, to stand out, to bring flavour to the bland world we live in:

Let me tell you why you are here. You're here to be salt-seasoning that brings out the God-flavors of this earth. If you lose your saltiness, how will people taste godliness? You've lost your usefulness and will end up in the garbage.

Here's another way to put it: You're here to be light, bringing out the God-colors in the world. God is not a secret to be kept. We're going public with this, as public as a city on a hill. If I make you light-bearers, you don't think I'm going to hide you under a bucket, do you? I'm putting you on a light stand. Now that I've put you there on a hilltop, on a light stand—shine!

Matthew 5:13–15 (*The Message*)

I really like Alan Scott's way of unpacking this in his book *Scattered Servants*:

The church you see is not peripheral to the culture; it's essential for the culture. You are a city on a hill. You are the light of the world. Raised up in the city; raised up for the city. The city doesn't make sense without the church, and the church doesn't make sense without the city. We are made visible to show forth a model of cultural renewal.[29]

The Early Church had great influence on those around them. Some were inspired by the way that they shared everything they had, and decided to join this new community (then known as 'The Way'). The religious leaders were uncomfortable and got the disciples arrested; others were offended and set out to destroy this embryonic movement. Whether the apostles and the Early Church brought inspiration, offence or discomfort, they were definitely influential.

I believe this is essential in fulfilling the four key areas required for the local church. You can have the greatest moments of *encounter*; you can regularly *gather* a group of people and help them *grow* in their Christian faith; but if there is no *influence* and no one is inspired, offended or uncomfortable about what you are doing, you have just become a club for your members.

The great commission that Jesus gave His followers was to go and make disciples of all nations, not to find a handful and then stop. Christians are meant to be influential. The Church is meant to be influential.

> The church, you see, is not peripheral to the world; the
> world is peripheral to the church.
> Ephesians 1:23 (*The Message*)

The question we should be asking ourselves is, if our church was to disappear off the face of the earth tomorrow, would the community around us notice we were gone? (Also a worthwhile question: if the community around us were to vanish overnight, would our church notice?)

We carry something more than a club or a charity or a community: we carry the very Spirit of God, and it should be vibrant and infectious. The local church should be the talk of its town, village or city – not because the coffee tastes better than the local coffee shop, or the worship band has the best sound, but because it is making a difference to the very community it serves. Any community served by a church should be a better place to be, simply because that church is there.

I was recently encouraged by this when, due to a diary clash, my colleagues and I were unable to attend a town-wide meeting of various local agencies. The lady running the meeting sent me an email to ask if there was a better date I could make, because 'if Freedom Church are unable to make it, then there is little point meeting up.' I want that to be the story for every church – that your local community will want regular input from their local church because they know it is a place of great influence and service.

People influence people

Imagine deliberating over whether or not to make a large purchase. You consider all the options, weigh up the pros and cons, check the prices and so on. Advertising may have pointed you towards the product, but whether you purchase it or not will often depend on people. The helpful sales assistant in the shop tells you how it will change your life; your friend says you deserve it; your neighbour has the old model; your spouse gives you the green light to stick it on the credit card and worry about it later... ultimately, people influence people.

I believe everyone can influence someone. We each have the ability to influence others. And more importantly, as Christians, we are to be Jesus-centred, Spirit-filled influencers – which is a great responsibility to carry.

The ability for one individual to make such an impact on the world so quickly has never been easier. It really is the era of the influencer. Media personality Kylie Jenner, who has something in the region of 30 million followers on social media, once posted a tweet expressing her indifference towards another platform. Immediately, Snapchat's stock fell by 7%, losing $1.3 billion in a matter of minutes. That's influence.

But you don't need to be a model with millions of followers or millions of dollars to make an impact. You don't even need a social media account. Yes, the crowd has always been impressed by money, fame and power, but each one of us has the ability to influence the world we inhabit, starting with those nearest to us. It doesn't have to be a big thing: smile at your colleagues; send hand-written cards; give your kids some of your time; offer to help... anyone; tip generously; say thank you and mean it; find out people's names and use them; collect up all the empty tea cups at work and wash them up without anyone asking; look people in the eye when you speak to them; listen when people are speaking to you... really *listen*; turn your phone off when eating with others... these small suggestions create huge influence. If you still don't believe you can influence others, then park your car in the middle of a road during rush hour and go for a coffee. When you get back, you will have influenced a lot of now very angry road users. (You may also end up with your car being towed away, so I'm not really recommending this one – but you get the point.)

I really do believe that *everyone can influence someone*.

When preaching what we now call the Sermon on the Mount, Jesus Himself said:

> let your good deeds shine out for all to see, so that everyone
> will praise your heavenly Father.
> Matthew 5:16

Jesus didn't say we should shy away from public opinion and hide our influence; He wants us to shine, and shine brightly. Remember that you carry influence and that every good deed you do will point people back to your Father God.

Our churches should be places of influence, but we need to remember that our churches are bigger than our Sunday meetings. We are here to serve the world and expand the rule and reign of Jesus our King. We believe in a God who is interested in our everyday needs, our neighbours and those in every sphere of our society, not just in singing nice songs or preaching with passion. Our churches are also more influential than the community projects and outreach that we deliver through a huge amount of effort.

The *people* in our churches are hugely influential. Why do you think companies online want to harvest our data? Because our details are valuable to them for directly, specifically and purposely marketing their products for us to buy. Churches often spend much of their time trying to get their crowd of people to 'buy into' the church programme and activities ('Sign up for this rota; join this team; come to this meeting') when, actually, we are called to send the church out into the world. I love how Alan Scott puts it:

> *Our calling and mission is to carry the kingdom beyond the church into the heart of culture. As sent people, the core of the church is no longer defined as those who support the structure of church, but those who are transforming culture as church.*[29]

It is great to gather – an important part of building culture and community – but our purpose in encountering, gathering and growing is to influence the world around us so that other people can encounter God for themselves. That is the great commission in action. If all we are saying to our church members is 'come to this event' or 'serve for this activity', then we are potentially reducing their influence in the world where God placed them.

Rick Warren writes that every member of a church should have their service to the church and their mission to the world.[30] The church gathering should be the place that launches us back into the world where we exist 99% of our week, not the activity that takes us out of our world and circle of influence. The kingdom of God is greater than any one church, and as followers of Jesus we get to expand the rule and reign of the King. Everywhere we go, Jesus is present in us. If we only ever gather all together in one space, then the very light that Jesus called us to shine out will only be for the benefit of those who already have a relationship with God. The people in our churches are incredible, but so are the people that haven't discovered their creator God yet. That's why we need to be building up our churches and sending them out in the power of the Holy Spirit, just as Jesus sent out His disciples (see Luke 10 and Matthew 10).

I remember being asked by a member of my leadership team if it was OK for them to get involved with the Big Lunch initiative, a national campaign to bring communities together over food. The event would be on a Sunday and it would mean them missing church that weekend. Instead, they would be closing down the road that they lived on and inviting the whole of their street to have a meal together. A great opportunity for influence! To lose your influence because you are too busy attending a meeting about being influential makes absolutely no sense to me.

As we have said already, gathering together is hugely important – but we often demand attendance through guilt (whether we realise it or not). Guilt will only reduce people's influence and future potential. Tell their stories and celebrate what they are doing as they bring light into the dark space where God has placed them. Encourage them to shine even brighter. Just like a city on a hill.

Influence goes beyond the church walls

My background in church work stems from a church that got heavily involved in the needs of the estate it served. We were in the middle of a neighbourhood known as Shepway Estate on the edge of Maidstone in Kent. It was a place of great need, but our involvement as a church was minimal for many years until one of the church members, Dave, decided to give up his job and serve the local community. I was only a teenager at the time, so my memory and understanding of this is kind of hazy, but I remember that it changed the church. We went from a 'nice middle-class church' with cars, careers and cheque books to having single parent families, kids that didn't want to engage and people that didn't know the unwritten church 'rules' (such as when to stand and when to be silent). I am sure it brought great challenges to those leading the church, but from where I sat, mainly on the back row as a teenager, it brought so much life to the church. It was inspiring and I loved it. Over the next few years, I got more involved with the work that church was doing until I left school and started working as their Schools and Community Worker, working with many of the same families and the same young lads that didn't want to engage with life and school, let alone the local church. The passage from Isaiah 61 became almost a life mantra for me: to bind up the broken-hearted; to bring good news to the poor. I wanted to make a difference.

They were formative years with some great memories, but the highlights for me were always watching people find faith and flourish. Volunteers from the church, who had never done anything like this before, stepped up to serve by filling in forms for people who had left school but were unable to write. As the volunteers realised that they had something to offer, they began to feel more valued and understand the influence and authority they carried. Then there were the families we were helping – the teenage mum on a limited budget, the addict, the homeless, the boy at risk of exclusion from school – all realising that these church people loved them and that they too could also have a relationship with God for themselves. Lives transformed – that's influence. But when those same people that had received help and found a new relationship with God then offered to make refreshments after church on Sunday, clean up gardens around the estate, make cakes for the coffee morning on a Wednesday, serve the broken-hearted and lead them into community and eventually into faith... that was a whole new level of influence. Sitting here now and remembering those moments brings tears to my eyes – I love that so many lives could benefit from the willingness of one small church to get its hands dirty and influence its local community. Dave is still faithfully serving those in need, and unsurprisingly went on to receive an MBE for his work in the local community.

After my time in Shepway, I moved to Rustington in West Sussex to embark on a new adventure of marriage to the beautiful Lottie (whom I had met while serving on the children's team together at Spring Harvest in Skegness – but that's another story!). Although I moved to another county, my involvement in community work didn't stop. I got stuck into my new church, who were already involved with their community through schools work and an annual play scheme. Then the church inherited an old chapel in the middle of a challenging housing estate (as you do). It was too small for us to fit everyone in on a Sunday, so I was tasked with looking at how we might utilise the building in other ways. With all that I'd learned from Shepway, I had plenty of ideas.

But I had no idea what was about to happen.

It was one of those moments you don't forget. I was sitting in my office when I got a phone call from a government project known as Sure Start, working to give young children and families a better start in life. 'Hi, Sim... we were wondering if we could knock down the old chapel and build a brand-new building in its place?'

I had no words. This was not at all what I was expecting. After various meetings, we agreed that Sure Start could knock down our old inherited Brethren chapel and build the Wickbourne Centre – a large hall that would seat around 150 people, with training rooms, counselling rooms, a commercial kitchen, a 65-place nursery, a crèche and toy library and, most importantly as far as I was concerned, a coffee shop.

A brand-new £1.3 million community centre, paid for by Sure Start, was handed over to the church.

True story.

That facility has enabled Arun Church to have huge influence in that community and beyond for the last 15 years. They run the nursery and coffee shop, and provide youth work for the town from that centre. Alpha courses, youth events, community programmes, toddler groups, health initiatives and much more – all because of a miraculous gift. Of course, the building is great... but it is still about the *people*. When I go back to the Wickbourne Centre and see all the people – some still on staff, but many volunteering – who have benefitted from the facility over the years, it brings great joy. They are a bright, bright light into that community.

I love to share stories like this because I believe the Church has a responsibility both individually and corporately. As individuals, we need to consider what we can do to influence the community we serve. We can all make a difference in the way that we treat people and show love and kindness in our workplace, in the family home and at the school gate. But sometimes, as the local church, we need to work together in delivering a specific project to provide a greater impact on a need that our community might face.

Freedom Church were actively involved in donating food to the local food bank in the next town when I received their annual report, saying they were feeding hundreds of people from our town. This was a real surprise to me, as I did not realise there was a need. I gave them a call and spoke to the manager there, and it turns out there was a lot of 'hidden hunger' in Romsey that we were totally unaware of. I knew we were donating a lot of food, but had no idea that a lot of those same tins were being returned to families on our very doorstep. After speaking with other church leaders in the area, all local churches committed to forming a new food bank, which opened in 2016. Since then, the wonderfully generous people of our town have donated tons of food. Dozens of volunteers have collected, sorted and stored the food, while even more volunteers have sat with clients in time of distress and great need and helped by providing emergency food provision. Hundreds of families have benefitted because of the Church standing together and shining light in the darkness.

I think we need to move beyond this mindset of any project being community-run *or* church-run. It doesn't have to be one or the other. The Church needs to continue to be those scattered servants that are volunteering in the library, listening to children read in the primary school, serving on the board of the carnival, helping to run a lunch club for the elderly or providing soup for the homeless in winter. Regardless of which agency is taking the credit for the project, we can still fully participate and celebrate this important contribution. Whether large, visible, corporate projects or silent service of those in need, the Church can, and should, have great influence in the community it serves.

> And the King will say, 'I tell you the truth, when you did it to one of the least of these my brothers and sisters, you were doing it to me!'
> Matthew 25:40

This is a great reminder from Jesus, who regularly went out of His way to help those on the fringes of society. Let's be challenged by this to do what we do not for personal gain, or to impress our friends or our followers online, but to consider that everything we do to 'the very least of these', we are doing it for God.

In helping the poor, needy and downtrodden, we are visibly preaching the gospel. Our kindness and compassion should reveal the person of Jesus.

Love and truth

You might be familiar with these famous words often attributed to Mother Teresa:

> People are often unreasonable, irrational, and self-centered.
> Forgive them anyway.
> If you are kind, people may accuse you of selfish, ulterior

motives. Be kind anyway.

If you are successful, you will win some unfaithful friends
and some genuine enemies. Succeed anyway.

If you are honest and sincere people may deceive you.
Be honest and sincere anyway.

What you spend years creating, others could destroy
overnight. Create anyway.

If you find serenity and happiness, some may be jealous.
Be happy anyway.

The good you do today, will often be forgotten.
Do good anyway.

Give the best you have, and it will never be enough.
Give your best anyway.

In the final analysis, it is between you and God. It was never
between you and them anyway.[31]

Now, I don't like to disagree with the great Mother Teresa, but I'd like to add a little 'P.S.' When I look at Jesus, I see that He would have compassion for those in need, but He would also challenge their behaviour. He would perform the miracle for the lame man, and then tell him to go and sin no more. He would rescue the woman caught in adultery, but then challenge her life choices.

As a church with a calling to influence, we are called to love, but we are not called to simply be nice. Our mission is not only to help people: it is love *and* truth. Our mission is to fill heaven, to reconnect God with His children. It doesn't seem right to celebrate the feeding of families, people becoming debt-free, families reunited, poverty overcome and relationships restored if we have not also given them an opportunity to hear the good news of Jesus. To do that we might have to use our influence to act justly *and* speak up.

I have heard some people use this argument against the

'social gospel', to opt out of caring for those in need because that is supposedly not our mission or our mandate. Personally, I don't believe the message of Jesus gives us that option. We are called firstly to make disciples, but service to others is part of our responsibility as disciples. I understand that each church will have its own gifting and part to play, and that not every church can run a large community project, but we can all participate in the world we live in somehow. We can all influence someone.

May we never compromise the gift we have been given, but be white-hot on both our community involvement and our preaching of the gospel. May we never become complacent about either.

Influence through partnership

The mission is bigger than you. It is bigger than me. It is bigger than our church or the local community we are endeavouring to influence.

It is the *great commission*, not a little mission for us to have a go at if we want to, and if it doesn't work, to simply shrug our shoulders. Jesus says, 'Go and make disciples of all nations.'

All nations.

And in case we weren't quite clear on that, He repeats Himself in His final pep talk to His followers (Acts 1:8) to tell people everywhere: 'in Jerusalem, throughout Judea, in Samaria, and to the ends of the earth.'

The ends of the earth.

That's a big vision. Probably bigger than most churches can handle.

Fortunately, the Church isn't restricted to your church or my church. There is a worldwide Church, which is *massive*. Billions of people belong to the Church, and it is in every nation of the world. It is His Church.

I believe we need to get a bigger vision of the Church if we want to fulfil this vast mission. You can't answer the call to the great commission single-handedly as one local church – and if you try, you will be disappointed very quickly. We can achieve so much more when we partner with others – both in our local community and all around the world. Embrace your wider Church family: partner with other churches in the community, partner with other Christian organisations around the nation, or partner with mission agencies overseas.

Going global

The world is vast and the mission is huge, but our ability to connect and communicate is greater now than at any other time in our history. The UK Church used to be one of the main centres of sending missionaries around the world to the forgotten places. Our ancestors got into boats with the risk of never returning. They would often spend years with tribes, learning new languages, translating Scripture or connecting across cultures. Today, the ability to travel is greater, the risk to health and family is lower, and yet it seems that the lack of risk has ironically reduced the number of those being sent to other nations.

But regardless of whether or not we are the ones to physically travel to 'the ends of the earth', we can still partner and influence together. There are some astonishing organisations around the world and in our own nation that create opportunities for partnership. For a number of years, I have been a trustee for Links International, set up by Norman and Grace Barnes in the 1970s to link together all the various projects and organisations they met over their visits to developing nations. This organisation still works in over 60 nations, supporting micro-enterprises, community healthcare, and often working in partnership with a local church or helping to plant one if one does not exist in that area.

As a church, we may not always be able to send teams and travel ourselves, but we can partner with others through prayer and funding. A relatively small amount of money can make a huge impact in a developing nation. On my first trip to Uganda, we arrived in Wobulenzi to be shown the work of ServeDirect, a charity that was founded by members of our church. We were shown the school with its 600 children (400 of whom stay on site as boarders), and were then taken to The Rock, a health clinic that serves the local community (the nearest hospital is a long way away). As we arrived, they were dealing with an emergency childbirth. A young expecting mother had gone into labour and was experiencing complications. They managed to deliver the baby, but there was serious concern that damage may have been caused due to lack of oxygen. As a church pastor, I was asked to come into the makeshift labour ward and pray for this beautiful, silent baby while the staff at the centre arranged for the mother to go to the nearest hospital. The plan was to send her on the back of a motorbike with her newborn son – a long distance for anyone, but for someone who had just given birth, that would have been horrendous. As a team we were able to get hold of a car and get her transported to the hospital more comfortably, where mother and baby were eventually deemed to be in good health.

Having just witnessed this scenario, the team I was travelling with asked the staff at the clinic what we could do to make a difference. Travelling by motorbike (or 'boda boda' as they are known) is really common in many parts of Africa where transport is so limited. We discovered that you can get 'bush ambulances', which are simple stretchers that fit onto the back of a boda boda, but they cost money and the charity had not deemed this a priority. The team had a quick discussion and agreed that between us all we could help with the purchase of a bush ambulance. A few weeks later we received an email with a picture of a shiny new bush ambulance, with members of The Rock trying it out with huge smiles on their faces. That piece of equipment has now been used numerous times to help transport people safely to hospital.

Together, we can make a difference. That's influence: one small act having a huge impact.

In 2015, The Cinammon Network created a 'Faith Action Audit' of the UK to measure how influential the Church was and the difference it was making to the nation. Its latest updated report reveals that the Church in the UK is providing over £3 billion in services to the nation, having over 5 million interactions with people each year through almost 200,000 volunteer roles.[32] Whether or not your local community would notice if your church closed tomorrow, the nation would definitely notice if the whole Church decided to close tomorrow.

In their book *Unleashed*, Gavin and Anne Calver encourage the Church to recognise its potential to make an impact:

> *Wherever we find ourselves that place is where we can make a difference for Christ... We must believe that our part is worthwhile and wherever we find ourselves – from the classroom, to the workplace, to the family dinner table, to the nightclub or the football pitch – we need to share something of the story of Jesus.*[33]

Partnering with unbelievers

Many churches run community projects with non-Christian agencies, such as youth work for the local council, education for pupils at risk of exclusion, or even health and wellbeing programmes. Some churches have created separate charities for their community work, to separate out the risk and enable them to gain funding – which may be otherwise restricted by their church's endeavors to advance the Christian faith. This may make partnering with non-Christian organisations a bit more straightforward, though some might see it as bending the rules to make it work. Others might suggest that workarounds like this are sensible and a win-win. Others still would say we shouldn't ever be 'unequally yoked with unbelievers' (2 Cor. 6:15), if that is their interpretation of that scripture. I remember one lady in a previous church who used this very verse to support her refusal to contribute to a project we were developing in partnership with the local council. We're bound to disagree on some things, but there are two principles that I believe are really important when working with other agencies as a local church.

First: be transparent about your beliefs.

It may be obvious to you what you believe as a church, but be upfront with your purpose. This is going back to our earlier discussion around our WHY as a church. The Church needs to be transparent about what it is there for. Otherwise it becomes a thin end of the wedge and our values get lost as we chase various funding streams (and before we know it we are a substantial charity that has a small church attached to it). Sadly, this really does happen. There are a number of churches that have a handful of church staff delivering their apparent core purpose, but they will also be employing dozens of extra staff to run their community activities. These activities are great at building bridges into our communities, but we have to be careful that our great commission does not get lost in the process. Let's be upfront about our purpose, making our beliefs clear to everyone who joins the team, and to any organisations that we partner with. That way, no one can say months down the line that they were unaware of our Christian faith and values.

Second: find the overlap. When we partner with other agencies, there will be some form of documentation to outline what each party will provide (and include any financial details). When we worked with Sure Start in West Sussex, we did not agree on everything – but we did agree that we wanted to provide young families with a great start in life. We found an overlap between our different purposes. Our reasons for doing the project were different, but we found some common ground where we could work together.

It is important that we make it clear how we want to partner, explaining what we will and won't do, ensuring there is good understanding from both parties. Discovering and articulating the overlap where you can work together will save frustration later on. Again, it's important in our partnerships that we stay true to our purpose as the local church.

Christians Against Poverty

There are lots of astounding Christian organisations out there, but I am a big fan of Christians Against Poverty (CAP) and the clarity that they have about their Christian faith. Founded by John Kirkby in 1996, they only work in partnership with local churches and have made it very clear to potential funders that they will not receive funding that restricts them from sharing the message of Jesus to those who find themselves in serious debt. This has cost them financially, but they have grown steadily into an international organisation that is well respected by many financial institutions. Working with hundreds of churches around the UK they have seen thousands of people become debt-free. Many of those people have come to faith and found true freedom.

It is possible to work in partnership as a church, but we need to be clear about our beliefs and purpose.

Freedom Church started working with CAP a few years ago, and it has been wonderful to share in their story of lives being transformed. Our team (mainly made up of volunteers) visit people in their homes, hear their situation and offer the services of CAP and the opportunity for prayer. It is rarely turned down. A number of those clients have started coming along to church because of the relationship that they've built with their volunteer befriender. We aren't just working to help people sort out their debt – we're also taking God's grace and love with us at the same time. Several clients have commented that after the home visits, they felt that there was hope and assurance through the support and prayer that we offer, as well as the help in becoming debt-free.

Partnering with other churches

Jesus did not want His Church to be fragmented, creating its own empires and brands. He wanted us to be united. One Church. His Church.

> I pray that they will all be one, just as you and I are one—as you are in me, Father, and I am in you. And may they be in us so that the world will believe you sent me.
> John 17:21

When we are united in our mission, we provide the world with a better image of what heaven looks like. That's why we it's so important that we partner and work together. It means we will get the job done more effectively, and it will reveal to the world how beautiful the Bride of Christ can be. As the saying goes: if you want to go fast, go on your own; if you want to go far, walk with others.[34]

Ultimately, when it comes to working in partnership, there is only one Church. It is His Church. We are temporary participants in this great history of the Church community that began 2,000 years ago as 'the Early Church', and still thrives in a variety of expressions around the world today. We are still one Church. When Jesus returns to this earth, He won't be choosing His favourite church to visit – He will be coming back for His Bride, the whole Church.

The influence of the Church is significantly reduced when we squabble over internal disputes. We can get sidetracked by various issues and the voice of the Church dissipates. I believe it is so important that, in our localities, we find ways to work together in a meaningful way.

The Church in the UK today is more culturally and ethnically diverse than ever. There are Chinese churches, Iranian churches, Turkish churches, Polish churches, Black, Asian and Minority Ethnic (BAME) churches and many others. I love the diversity we can celebrate in the UK and in the Church – it is a healthier and much more accurate representation of God's people. The work of the Evangelical Alliance and their One People Commission[35] in recent years has been significant in connecting different church leaders and their congregations, to help churches understand that we are better together. Our influence becomes broader and our voice gets louder as we speak well of each other, whatever our differences might be.

It's so important we remember that we are not in competition with other churches, but offer alternative styles and approaches to worship. We are working side by side for the same God. If there is a competition, it is for souls – to see as many people as possible saved. It does not matter which church they feel more comfortable in. The point is that they come to know Jesus. If another church in our town is growing – great! Rather than competing, let's be looking at other churches and learning from them. If they are doing something well, find out more. Borrow ideas. Get in touch and have a chat. If we can help each other get better, everyone wins.

Having just said how much I love diversity, and the importance of recognising we are one Church, I don't usually find that having joint church services works brilliantly well. One church provides the music, one provides the venue, one provides the speaker and one provides the refreshments: it sounds lovely in theory, but it is often simply a politer version of our real selves, just trying to get through the sung worship and make it a 'unified success'. Unity doesn't necessarily mean 'everyone in the same building at the same time'. But we can always pray together and serve the needs of our community together. There are not that many different ways to feed the hungry or provide shelter for the homeless. We may not be able to do everything together (after all, there is usually a reason why we have our separate spaces and traditions), but we should always speak well of each other.

It is not our Church. It is His.

When we speak badly of another church, we are throwing mud at the Bride of Christ. We want the Bride to look as beautiful as possible, to glow like a lamp on a stand or a city on a hill – that all who see her will know she is something really special.

The Church – a place of great influence.

Under
the bonnet

Yes, you do have a system for that

Language can be a funny thing, and easily misunderstood. 'Let's eat Grandma' and 'Let's eat, Grandma' are two very different statements – and one is life-threatening for poor Grandma.

I had my own experience of this when I was completing a written assignment. I needed to get the document proof read to ensure I was being as accurate as possible (particularly when it came to spelling). One of the comments I got back from my proof reader, Lynda, was that I was being inconsistent with how I was capitalising the word 'church'. Very graciously, she explained to me that it's all to do with proper nouns and common nouns (don't worry, this will make sense in a sec). A proper noun should be capitalised as it is the name of a specific location ('I am going to St Peter's Church today'). An individual church, more generally speaking, is referred to by the lower-case common noun, even if a specific one is inferred ('going to church').

Then there is the Church – the universal Bride of Christ, a worldwide community of God's people throughout the ages. It is not specific in location or organisation, but it is not *a* church – it is *the* Church. His Church.

We need to care for our church systems, but Jesus didn't die for 'the system'; He died for the souls that the system is there to serve. But if we don't look after the trellis, then the vine will have no structure on which to flourish. So, while keeping our 'WHY' in mind, let's take a look at the 'HOW', and think about the systems of church – how things work.

This is the Haynes Manual part of the book, which explains what goes on under the bonnet of the car and shows how everything works. If we're honest, lots of us won't be all that interested in what happens under the bonnet – we just want the car to get us to work and back home again without breaking down in rush hour. But others of us love to tinker with car engines to make them more efficient. If we had no mechanics, our cars would eventually stop working. Like the trellis for the vine and the engine for the car, how a church works is important – but it doesn't necessarily need to be *seen*. We want it to work reliably and effectively, but how it works can stay under the bonnet.

According to Craig Groeschel, Senior Pastor of Life.Church: 'If your organisation has a problem, it is a system problem!'[36] Whether you love them or hate them, your systems will be your biggest problem. What you allow and what you create will be your system. We all have them – in our homes, workplaces and in our churches.

Not everyone loves a good system, but some can't get enough of a beautiful spreadsheet or a colourful Gantt chart (if you don't know what a Gantt chart is, then you are probably not one of those people). A member of my team recently expressed their love of the book of Leviticus, one of the trickiest bits of the Bible to understand within our modern culture. The reason that they loved this awkward book so much? Because it created very clear-to-follow rules for the people of the day – rules of who does what, and how things should work. It's a book of systems created by Moses to ensure the people of Israel worked well as a community living in challenging conditions. It was a Haynes Manual for early Jewish living.

Systems are simply the way that we organise ourselves, and although at one level this is very practical, it is also an expression of our culture reflecting the 'why' we do what we do by the very *way* that we do it.

I heard a story of a lady who every Christmas would take the legs off the turkey before placing the legs back in the roasting pan and putting the whole bird in the oven. One year, her teenage daughter finally asked her, 'Why do you take the legs off the turkey before you put it in the oven?' The mum had no idea, and simply explained that that was how her mum had done it when she was growing up, and so she just did it the same way that she had always seen it done. So over their Christmas lunch, she asked her own mum why she cut the legs off the turkey before roasting it. Grandma laughed as she replied, 'When I was first married, our oven was too small to fit the turkey, so I would cut off the legs so that it would fit in the oven.'

Our needs create systems, our systems create behaviour, our behaviour creates habits, and our habits create culture. But our church habits and systems, if never reassessed against Scripture, can create an unhealthy culture where we do things simply because that is the way we have always done them. Following rules without question ultimately creates religion.

> Don't let anyone capture you with empty philosophies and high-sounding nonsense that come from human thinking and from the spiritual powers of this world, rather than from Christ.
>
> Colossians 2:8

The Church is God's plan – His idea. Jesus said to Peter, 'I will build my church', but He also went on to say that He would give him the keys to the kingdom to empower His people on earth (Matt. 16:18–19). While it is God's Church and He will build it, we all have a part to play in helping it grow. As Paul said, he planted the seed, his friend Apollos watered it, but it is God who made it grow (1 Cor. 3:6).

To create space to enable all kinds of people to participate and play their part in God's great story of the Church, we need effective systems that work but stay under the bonnet.

Keeping it hidden

The purpose of a car is to transport people, but you need an engine to do it. No matter how nice the seats, tyres and steering wheel might be, you're not going to buy a car that doesn't have an engine. If it can't fulfil its purpose in transporting people from one place to another, it's redundant. In the same way, the Church's purpose is to be a vibrant community of believers and point people to God, but it needs an engine to keep things going. I know many people will say that surely the engine is the Holy Spirit in this analogy, but I would suggest that the Holy Spirit is the fuel that powers the engine, while we are responsible for ensuring that we do things in the right way while still prepared for the Spirit to do what only He can do.

We have a responsibility to keep the engine of a church maintained, but at the same time it should remain unseen. The behind-the-scenes activity of a church is simply a mechanism of creating space for people to ENCOUNTER God for themselves, to GATHER regularly, to GROW in their faith and INFLUENCE their families and friends. When it is done right, no one even needs to know that it is there – and that's the way it should be. And whether we call it the back office, the staff team or the engine room, it is still an important part of the church.

It's useful to have clarity on how things work, so that each one of us can be fully part of our church communities and flourish. For example, I mentioned earlier that at Freedom Church we have a system of membership, which we call partnership. To be a partner of the church, you invest your time, talent and treasure: you turn up regularly (time), serve in some capacity (talent) and give financially towards the work of the church (treasure). It's a simple, self-selecting system, but it is still a system. This helps people joining our church know what is expected of them and it also helps those involved with leadership to know who is committed to the life of the church.

God loves administrators

We don't say it enough in our churches, but people who can organise and administrate should be celebrated. It's a gift! When talking to His disciples, Jesus Himself said, 'who would begin construction of a building without first calculating the cost to see if there is enough money to finish it?' (Luke 14:28).

Have you ever had an idea that you were struggling to get off the ground, but then someone came along with the practical know-how to make it happen? Ideas only become reality when someone starts to do something. Every idea, every book that is written, music composed, play or film script produced, artwork created, will always stay hidden unless somebody helps make it become something tangible. Creativity is right at the heart of God, the creator of all things. But good ideas require administration and application for them to exist. Administration and management systems take great ideas, create systems to achieve them, and then ensure there is follow-through and feedback to improve those systems. Book concepts only become real when publishers get hold of them. Script ideas become films when producers and distributors give their energy and time. Business concepts take off when financial investors sow their money. There is no such thing as a self-made success story. They will always have had support from family, friends, business colleagues, customers, investors. For dreams to become reality, we need administrators. We need systems.

In the Old Testament, Pharaoh needed Joseph (Gen. 41). Joseph was a man who heard God through dreams, but then created a system of storing crops for seven years and then distributing them evenly for seven years after that to ensure that the nation survived a disastrous famine. A food distribution system.

Moses needed Jethro (Exod. 18). Moses was exhausted with all the requests of the people, so Jethro suggested a system of delegation to place leaders over groups of thousands, hundreds, fifties and tens. The load was shared. A management system.

The city of Jerusalem needed Nehemiah (Neh. 2–6). Nehemiah was a cupbearer to the king, but he was also an efficient administrator. He assessed the broken walls of the city, gathered leaders together, delegated tasks, managed the finances, dealt with the opposition, formed teams... and in 52 days the walls had been rebuilt. A construction system.

Every part of your church activity will need a system. If you produce a weekly news sheet, you will need a system for collating information, designing, printing and distributing. If you run a children's programme, you will need volunteer schedules, training, safety checks and safeguarding policies – all before you start considering what your teaching programme might be. If you have a building, you will need a budget, a maintenance plan, key holders, health and safety assessments. If you receive money, you will need to account for that income, present reports and manage expenditure. If you have church staff, you will need to have systems for employment, payment, management and training.

It may not be particularly exciting, but for our churches to run smoothly, we really do need efficient and effective systems. The great news is today you can get your hands on various different programs and platforms that can help you achieve a lot of these things – apps, database templates, training and so on. And if the systems are running smoothly, you can focus on what is really important: the people and the mission.

Healthy leadership, healthy church

The first hallmark of the Early Church that we looked at in the opening section was their commitment to the apostles' teachings. The role of the Early Church leadership team was essential in developing that early community into a movement that spread out across the known world at that time – an incredible achievement. There were plenty of mistakes made by this ragtag group of leaders that Jesus invested into for three years, but their passion for the gospel message, and for the Jesus they served, was unstoppable.

There was disagreement about the involvement of Gentiles (non-Jews) in their group; there were challenges about how money was managed; not everyone got on, and some relationships broke down; some thought the leaders should serve those in need and some thought they should spend their time praying and preparing the message. Not much has changed in 2,000 years.

Healthy leadership in the local church is absolutely vital. Church leadership is more than just managing the systems that have been created: it is about seeking God for His divine direction, communicating clearly this God-given mission, and then developing and empowering people to put that great commission into practice.

I completely agree with John Maxwell in saying, 'everything rises and falls on leadership'[37]. A healthy church leader can take a disillusioned group of believers and give them life and direction. Likewise, a healthy congregation can be seriously damaged by leadership that wields power for its own gain. There is always a risk in leadership in that it can be misused, but a biblical, authentic, healthy, growing church needs clearly defined leadership.

I believe it is always worth taking a risk and empowering people to lead, believing in faith that God will use them, rather than endeavouring to keep control out of fear of what someone might do if they were to be given a position of responsibility in the local church. However, it is vital that we select people with the right character. The apostle Paul instructed Titus clearly about appointing local church leaders:

> A church leader is a manager of God's household, so he must live a blameless life. He must not be arrogant or quick-tempered; he must not be a heavy drinker, violent, or dishonest with money. Rather, he must enjoy having guests in his home, and he must love what is good. He must live wisely and be just. He must live a devout and disciplined life. He must have a strong belief in the trustworthy message he was taught; then he will be able to encourage others with wholesome teaching and show those who oppose it where they are wrong.
> Titus 1:7–9

Titus was not charged with setting up a voting system for leaders, or finding which people were the 'nicest' or most popular. Mandated qualities of those in leadership include honesty, faithfulness, hospitality, wisdom and discipline. Let's not be dismissive of them.

Developing leadership potential

As well having the right character attributes, a leader also needs to be competent in their role. A good character is not necessarily indicative of a strong leader.

Here are four steps that you may find helpful in spotting and developing potential leaders.

1. Identify

Don't assume that great leadership only happens at the front – in fact, it is rarely spotted on a platform. It's always interesting to see how a person behaves and treats other people when they think no one is looking. Look out for those who naturally gather groups of people around them. The way a leader speaks to those who can do nothing for them in return says a lot about their character. I do believe leadership can be developed in pretty much anyone, but many people have a natural leadership instinct, and a desire to lead others.

It's also good to be aware of your own unconscious bias, and consider people who are different to you (which means you may have to go outside of your comfort zone to find them in the first place!). Identify those who are quick to serve and have a desire to learn from others. Look for people who are willing to listen, and not just those who want to show you how amazing they are.

Some people will already have a desire or a calling to lead. As a young leader, I always felt slightly guilty for having this sense that God was calling me into church leadership. I thought it might sound fanciful, or even arrogant, so I kept quiet – and not having the opportunity to express my calling only made me feel frustrated.

2. Clarify

Once you have found someone with character, competency and a clear sense of calling, then it is important that this is clarified before giving them a leadership role. Ask other members of your leadership team what they think of the person that you have in mind. The important thing here is not the opinions of your team, as they will vary based on preference of leadership style, but to see if there is a consistent thread around their character or behaviour. If a large number of your team are uncomfortable, then don't pursue things any further. The chemistry of a leadership team working together is important. A new member creates a new team.

Pray about that person; seek God for clarity on whether they are a good fit for the role you have in mind (ask others to join you in prayer and see if God will give you a revelation about the individual). We can easily be impressed by someone's abilities, but the character that is sometimes masked is always more important. It is much easier to appoint into a leadership role than it is to remove someone from a position of responsibility. Take great care. It is far better to move forward slowly with the right character than to move fast with the wrong character. As Arthur Wallis puts it, 'Leadership flaws are always caused by character breakdown rather than gifting failure.'[38]

3. Opportunity

Once you have spotted someone that you think has potential, prayed about it and clarified it with other members of the leadership team, give that person an opportunity to express their leadership. The scale of the role is not important, just give them something to lead. It doesn't matter if it is organising the next church weekend or leading the midweek quiz night – just see how they do. Give them a task to complete that is realistic for their competency and experience. There is a big difference in being planted and being buried – in one you are expected to come back stronger and having grown.

Remember, you are still looking for great character, which is hard to see when someone is on their guard, but you can see it in their activity, in the way they treat people, how they respond to the new responsibility and ultimately in the fruit of their leadership.

Once the activity is completed, meet with them and assess the experience. As I mentioned before, the phrase 'people learn through experience' is simply not true. As a church leader I have seen people make the same mistakes over and over again; their repetitive experiences do not seem to develop any learning, or they would stop doing it. We learn through assessing the experiences that we have and adjusting what we do for next time. As you assess the potential leader you will also get a feel for how accountable they are, or how teachable of new ideas they might be.

4. Create trust

In his book *Five Dysfunctions of a Team*, Patrick Lencioni suggests that where there is no trust, there is no foundation on which to build a healthy team.[39] How do you create trust? By going first.

To create trust with another potential leader you need to show some weakness and vulnerability. Revealing something of your inadequacies or limitations will create a deeper relationship and greater trust. A show of strength breeds competition, but vulnerability breeds community.

People tend to live up to our expectations, so it's OK to have high expectations. Put your trust in someone and believe the best of them, and see what happens.

Clarity of roles

One of the most damaging situations in church leadership is when there is a lack of clarity over roles. I remember having a coffee with a young Bible college graduate who had just started working at a local church. He was excited about his new role, so I asked him to tell me what he was going to be doing. Within a couple of minutes it became clear that he did not know what his role was; he was unsure of the limitations of his authority and whether he was leading the church or assisting the voluntary eldership team. Within six months he left the church in frustration, and almost left the ministry entirely due to his disappointment and misunderstanding.

It has often been said that leadership is simply taking people from A to B. Leadership at one level is simple, but if you are not sure what is being asked of you, you will most likely cease operating out of fear, or react out of frustration. Neither are healthy for anyone, least of all a developing leader. Natural leaders will always find something to lead, and if they have no clarity then they will either lead in the wrong direction or with the wrong emphasis, or they will take their leadership gift and use it elsewhere.

Every church needs to have a clear leadership structure and for each person to have a clear role. If you can't articulate your role in a short sentence, then you need to seek clarification.

I believe in the church being led by a team of people for mutual support and accountability, but I also believe that it is important to know who leads that team. The senior leader has responsibility for owning the vision and the culture of the organisation, and isn't something you can outsource. It's a bit like the 'mumps and measles principle' – as a leader, if you say you have mumps but are actually carrying measles, then those following you will catch what you are carrying, not what you say you have. This is the same with culture and behaviour. If the leader says the church should pray but the leader never prays, we should not be surprised that the church doesn't pray. If we say the church should be generous but we are the last to offer to pay for a round of drinks, then our church will mirror our secret behaviour not our public declarations.

Pursue clarity in your church leadership team. Start by drawing up a chart if necessary, and a short description of each person's role. Regularly assess those in positions of leadership and ensure that people are still clear on what they are expected to do. Don't run away from titles. Give clarity for church leaders, whether paid roles or voluntary. Leadership is about the responsibility you carry, not about the tasks that need to be achieved.

Empowering others

Leadership is never about the one, it is always about the many. A healthy church will have a variety of leadership opportunities and needs, so it is essential that responsibility is delegated out clearly and carefully. Sometimes we drop too much responsibility onto unsuspecting volunteers, and it looks more like abdication than delegation. Alternatively, a church leader can empower a volunteer with a key responsibility and then continue interfering, which can lead to frustration all round. The biggest breakdowns in communication in any organisation are often because of a misunderstanding of the level of responsibility being handed over. Leaders need to clearly communicate exactly what they expect, and ensure there is full understanding from the person being delegated to.

In my understanding, there are four basic approaches to delegating:

- 'This is completely your project: you are fully in charge, you can make all the decisions, I only need to hear when the project is completed.'
- 'This is your project: you are fully in charge, but I would like regular updates as you proceed. I may need to make adjustments, but you will get all the credit for any success.'
- 'This my project, but I would like your help with it. I would like you to research some possible ways we could do this, come back to me, and then we will agree which option to go with.'
- 'This is my project, but I would like your help with it. I will give you clear instructions of what to do each step of the way. When each step is completed, come back to me and we will discuss the next.'

Show me a church leader that holds all the power and I will show you a small, unhealthy church. The church is a community that needs to share the great 'co-mission' and empower people – a place where each member can flourish in their God-given gifts. Leadership is one of those gifts.

When we take on new staff members at Freedom Church, we talk about this. The role of a church employee is not to run everything, but to empower more volunteers. I don't want our youth worker to be the only member of the youth team, running around providing all our young people's needs. I want them to be building a team of volunteers that can reach out to more young people and have a greater impact in our church and the local community. I want them to feel fully empowered to make the appropriate decisions required for them to fulfil their role, with the right budget, team and job description. I don't want them to do everything. I want them to enable others and share the responsibility, investing in others and watching them grow. Leadership in the church is there to build up the body of Christ so that His Church is beautiful, and the kingdom is advanced. Church leadership is always about the service of others. It is never about a position or a title. Jesus was the ultimate servant leader, who never pursued position but always set the best example, humble enough to wash His followers' dirty feet – even the feet of the one who would betray Him.

As we have already said, systems are important, but it is our attitude that matters most when it comes to leadership in the church. We are to 'have the same attitude that Christ Jesus had' (Phil. 2:5) in the way that we treat and speak to people. You can have the perfect church model, with a beautiful website, spectacular Sunday services... and a rotten attitude. You can also have a church that is quite scruffy and disorganised, but is led by people with an incredible love for God and His people.

Teams are powerful

Teams can achieve so much, but only when there is a clear purpose and each individual has an understanding of the part they play. Each person in a team works differently, with different expectations and aspirations. It's important to recognise this, and be aware of evolving dynamics. Every time someone leaves or joins a team, it is essentially a new team.

I think it's worth briefly considering a few key points about church leadership teams. Ideally, they should be small enough to fit round a table, with everyone engaged in both food and conversation. Yes, food – it's important for building relationships (it's also very enjoyable). Having said that, it's important to consider the size of the church when you develop a leadership team. Having a leadership team of eight when there is a Sunday congregation of twelve would be ridiculous. Likewise, having a membership of thousands led by a team of three would be unhealthy, unsustainable and unwise.

In a room full of leaders, you're going to have a lot of capable people who most likely have a variety of different approaches. That's why one person needs to create the agenda, steer the conversation, ensure there is space for everyone to be heard, and bring a conclusion with clear actions delegated appropriately. (The position of 'leader of leaders' (team leader) should never be about seniority or position, but about an extra level of responsibility and accountability.) The leadership structure needs to reflect the size of your church as it is now *and* what you hope for it to become. Think of leadership as the cork in the bottle: if you have a leadership structure and mindset that can only handle one hundred people, then that is the limit to which you will grow.

Tim Keller has written a really interesting article on 'Leadership and Church Size Dynamics', highlighting links between leadership and congregation size. For example, in a small church, everyone knows the pastor and will often expect that person to know all about them too; but in a much larger church, the leadership needs to be delegated out and the expectation of being known by the church leader is much less. The challenge comes when a church has a 'growth spurt', and most people no longer have the same access to the church leader that they once had (or if you move from a small church to a larger church and expect the same level of interaction).[40]

It's worth considering, therefore, how we can create structures of leadership suitable for our present congregation size and also for our future ambitions. One way to do this is to create an organisational chart that details the scale of church you would like to become, and then simply place the team that you presently have in a variety of roles and responsibility. You can then slowly move people out of their wider range of roles by empowering other people to volunteer (or take on employment) to focus on a specific area. For instance, if you are a smaller church, you may have one volunteer overseeing all your youth, children and families ministry – but as you grow, you may appoint volunteers for each specific area that specialise in that particular age group. The original volunteer may completely step aside, or choose to lead one area where their gifts are most suited.

The Jesus model of leadership

Church leadership is all about service of others. It is the Jesus way. It is never about power, position or prominence. Church organisation charts should be upside down with those called to lead at the very bottom, serving the church and enabling them to influence their families, workplaces and communities. It is always about Jesus. His example was to take enthusiastic and willing followers, show them how it's done, and empower them to do the work in His name.

Church leadership is a God-given calling, and if you have been blessed with leadership ability, take it seriously and invest in the gift that you have been given. But keep your heart and motives in the right place.

When Jesus' disciples were arguing over who was the greatest and would have the best seat in the house, Jesus put it like this, and I think He deserves the last word on this:

> You know that the rulers in this world lord it over their people, and officials flaunt their authority over those under them. But among you it will be different. Whoever wants to be a leader among you must be your servant, and whoever wants to be first among you must become your slave. For even the Son of Man came not to be served but to serve others and to give his life as a ransom for many.
> Matthew 20:25–28

Shhh! Don't talk about money

Let's be honest: when it comes to money in church, we are often too embarrassed to talk about it.

But money is an everyday reality for everyone, and if the Church isn't talking about it, where will people get their financial advice from?

I think it's important to touch on some of the basics, with the overarching principle that we should see money as an issue of stewardship, not ownership. When we stop thinking of our money and possessions as 'ours', it changes everything. After all, none of it is ours – it is all God's, and we are simply managing it for a season. Stewardship is something that God bestowed upon Adam and Eve in the Garden of Eden (Gen. 1:28; 2:15) – it is in the very fabric of humanity. What would happen if your church started handling its money as if it was all God's and not their own? What difference would it make if we started stewarding well that which we have been entrusted with?

The way we handle money makes a statement about what is important. What you spend your money on reflects the priorities that you hold as an individual, but the same is true of the Church. If all a church's money is spent on the building, then that is its priority; if it is all being spent on community activity, then that is its priority; if it is all spent on the youth programme, then that is its priority.

> Wherever your treasure is, there the desires of your heart will also be.
> Matthew 6:21

Have you noticed that, in this verse from Matthew 6, 'where your treasure is' comes before 'your heart'? The heart follows the treasure, not the other way round. If you want to love your spouse more, invest in them more.

What do we do with what we've got?

The Bible talks *a lot* about money. Jesus talked more about money than he did heaven and hell. In fact, the only thing Jesus talked about more than money is the kingdom of God – that is how important a subject it is. In the Gospel of Luke, roughly one in every seven verses talk about money. In 11 of the 39 parables, Jesus talked about money, including this one:

> **The Story About Investment**
> It's also like a man going off on an extended trip. He called his servants together and delegated responsibilities. To one he gave five thousand dollars, to another two thousand, to a third one thousand, depending on their abilities. Then he left. Right off, the first servant went to work and doubled his master's investment. The second did the same. But the man with the single thousand dug a

hole and carefully buried his master's money.

After a long absence, the master of those three servants came back and settled up with them. The one given five thousand dollars showed him how he had doubled his investment. His master commended him: 'Good work! You did your job well. From now on be my partner.'

The servant with the two thousand showed how he also had doubled his master's investment. His master commended him: 'Good work! You did your job well. From now on be my partner.'

The servant given one thousand said, 'Master, I know you have high standards and hate careless ways, that you demand the best and make no allowances for error. I was afraid I might disappoint you, so I found a good hiding place and secured your money. Here it is, safe and sound down to the last cent.'

The master was furious. 'That's a terrible way to live! It's criminal to live cautiously like that! If you knew I was after the best, why did you do less than the least? The least you could have done would have been to invest the sum with the bankers, where at least I would have gotten a little interest.

'Take the thousand and give it to the one who risked the most. And get rid of this "play-it-safe" who won't go out on a limb. Throw him out into utter darkness.'

Matthew 25:14–30 (*The Message*)

The first two servants are seen as good stewards and are invited to 'come and share [the] master's happiness!' (v23, NIV) – no longer a servant, but a partner with the land owner. This is God's class system.

But the one-talent servant (the servant with one thousand dollars in *The Message* translation) buried his gift and exposed his fear. He was afraid of his master. Why did the first two invest the talents and not hide them? Because they *knew* the master better. The last one was afraid because he did not know the master well. There is a direct connection between how we as followers of Jesus manage our money and how well we know the Master.

God doesn't mind us having stuff; He minds stuff having us. It's all about stewardship. What we think we own, we only have on loan.

> The earth is the LORD's, and everything in it.
> Psalm 24:1

We might default to thinking, 'It's my money, I earned it!' – but really we get to look after what belongs to God, and what He has given into our hands. We get to play, but it is all His.

As your church is faithful with little, God will give you more. I used to wonder why the servant with ten talents got the extra talent from the servant that hid his allocation, but now I believe it is because whoever stewards well will receive more, but those that steward poorly will receive none.

We all get something. We are all granted different resources, gifts, time and income. God may be just, but He does not have to be fair (see the parable of the vineyard workers in Matthew 20 if that sounds confusing!), but whatever our churches have been given, it is always more than zero.

Every church has a talent and a gift. Every church has something to offer. The million-dollar question (pardon the pun) is this: 'What are we going to do with what we've got?'

Maybe it's a historic building that has served the local community for hundreds of years – what are we going to do with what we've got?

A growing number of young families join the church – what are we going to do with what we've got?

We've been given a large piece of land to build a new church facility – what are we going to do with what we've got?

We receive a substantial legacy from a long-serving member of the church – what are we going to do with what we've got?

This is the purpose of Jesus telling the story about investment: that His Father rewards those who use well what they have been given.

What are you going to do with what you've got?

Money is very useful, but it's just a thing. It has no intrinsic power of its own, but used wisely it can do a lot of good. Money is both practical and very spiritual. We have a responsibility to be good stewards of what we have been given, but that doesn't mean we bury it in the ground, terrified of what God might do if we put our resources to work. Good stewardship of money should reflect the heart of God: never wasteful, but always generous.

Generosity to others

Money is powerful: it has been the downfall of business leaders, led to the breakdown of marriages, and created huge damage in churches. It's time we understand that money is not meant to stay in our hands or in our banks, but to be used as a tool to help others, forever moving from one person to another (maybe that's why it's called currency...?).

Healthy churches are always generous with their finances because they understand that everything they have is from God anyway. Let's be a generous Church in every way: generous with our time, generous with our talents, and generous with our treasure. If it is truly more blessed to give than to receive (Acts 20:35), then the key to becoming a blessed church is cultivating a heart of generosity. If you want to be more blessed, you will become more blessed when you become more generous.

In order to explain this, Jesus told the parable of the widow's offering. It's an often misunderstood passage of scripture, sometimes misused to suggest that we should give 100% of all we have to the church collection plate. But that's not the idea.

> Jesus sat down near the collection box in the Temple and watched as the crowds dropped in their money. Many rich people put in large amounts. Then a poor widow came and dropped in two small coins.
> Jesus called his disciples to him and said, 'I tell you the truth, this poor widow has given more than all the others who are making contributions. For they gave a tiny part of their surplus, but she, poor as she is, has given everything she had to live on.'
> Mark 12:41–44

Real generosity gives out of faith, not surplus. This woman may have been a widow with limited resources, but she had faith that what she was giving to was of good purpose. She put her trust in God, rather than her savings or her earning prospects. This parable is such a clear illustration of the reminder in 1 Samuel 16:7 that 'People judge by outward appearance, but the LORD looks at the heart.' We are often impressed by what we see, but Jesus was pointing out the widow's internal, unseen attitude. As Jesus speaks about prayer, giving and fasting (throughout Matthew 6), He continuously reminds us to do these things in private: to go into an inner room and pray, to give our gifts in private, and to wash our faces so no one knows when we have been fasting. Jesus is always more impressed by our hidden habits than our public performance.

Real generosity will change the life of our churches and the lives of other people in our communities. As a generous Church we are to answer the call of Matthew 25 – to feed the hungry, invite the stranger, provide clothing, care for the sick and visit the lonely. That is real generosity. When we encounter Jesus, He doesn't just overhaul our wallets to make us more generous, but He gives a new spirit that embraces every opportunity to be generous. This isn't just how we behave to others, it is our very worship to God Himself. How we treat others is our act of worship. Our generosity and extravagance in giving to 'the least of these' is directly connected to our love for God. I really do believe that the Church should be the most generous of all organisations on the planet, giving everything we have, as that is exactly what Jesus has done for us – His death on a cross in our place is the ultimate display of outrageous generosity. How much more should we be generous with the little that we have.

Giving to the church

I can feel everyone's discomfort as I write these words. *Do we have to talk about giving?* We understand the concept of stewardship and looking after what God has given to us as a church community, and we love the idea of being a generous church and reflecting the heart of God... but the whole 'church and giving' thing is always so awkward. It conjures up images of the excited preacher on TV shouting at us to give our money to God, so that we will be blessed – or, perhaps more likely in the UK, the silent, uncomfortable moment where the two-handled blue velvet bag is slowly passed from person to person without any eye contact whatsoever. How we handle the giving of money in church reveals so much about our church culture. Jesus spoke a lot about money, not because He was interested in money itself, but He knew that our relationship with money reveals something of our very nature.

So let's talk about it.

What does the Bible say about giving?

> Since you excel in so many ways—in your faith, your gifted speakers, your knowledge, your enthusiasm, and your love from us—I want you to excel also in this gracious act of giving... Let the eagerness you showed in the beginning be matched now by your giving. Give in proportion to what you have. Whatever you give is acceptable if you give it eagerly. And give according to what you have, not what you don't have.
>
> 2 Corinthians 8:7,11–12

I love the phrase Paul uses here: 'excel in this gracious act of giving'. That would be my dream for the Church around the world also. Imagine if every church excelled in this gracious act of giving, what an incredible, world-changing difference we could make!

Our financial giving in church is a test of our faith. The number ten in Scripture is often to describe a test (such as ten plagues; ten commandments; the ten lepers Jesus healed in Luke 17).

> Bring all the tithes into the storehouse so there will be enough food in my Temple. If you do,' says the LORD of Heaven's Armies, 'I will open the windows of heaven for you. I will pour out a blessing so great you won't have enough room to take it in! Try it! Put me to the test!'
>
> Malachi 3:10

We bring our finances to say that we are God's, and our priority is Him and Him alone. We put our trust in Him and His provision, and not our own earning capacity. Do we trust God, or do we trust our ability to earn money? Are we self-reliant or God-reliant? As a church, do we trust the giving capacity of our congregation, or God's promise that He will provide all our needs? Do we really believe that if we bring all that we can as a 'tithe into the storehouse' then He promises to pour out a blessing so great that 'you won't have enough room to take it in'?

Let's make our giving to the local church a declaration of our commitment, faith and thanksgiving – not because we feel guilty or obligated, or have a little extra in the bank that week. We give out of a love for God, regardless of our circumstances. Sometimes people don't want to give to the church because they don't agree with how it is being spent. I'd like to suggest something here: if you are not happy with how money is being spent, then ultimately you are not happy with the leadership of your local church. By all means arrange a conversation with your church leader if you have concerns, but don't stop giving. Your faith is in God and His provision, not in church leaders.

Practical challenges of giving

Let's be honest: this is a tricky area, and it doesn't necessarily work to have a blanket rule for giving. What about people in debt? What about people on low income? What about students? What about church members who are married to a non-believer? Does 'tithing' apply to net or gross income? Is it better to give every week into the offering as part of our regular worship, or set up a standing order, which perhaps feels less spiritual?

It comes down to our attitude. God is always more interested in the heart of a believer than in the amount that they give. He loves a person who gives cheerfully (2 Cor. 9:7), so let's be joyful about what we give away. What we give our money to reveals what is valuable to us, so what are we investing in?

If the church is the house of God, how we manage it reflects the owner of the house and how He is perceived by the world. If we are stingy and withholding, the world sees God as stingy and withholding. If we are generous and joyful about it – if we feast and celebrate occasionally – that's the God our community will see. Show me a healthy church and I will show you a church that has learnt the blessing that comes from giving.

Weathering the storm

The Church has always faced challenges.

The Church *began* in the midst of persecution. The Jewish leaders did not roll out a red carpet and welcome the members of the Early Church, or 'The Way' as it was known.

Those abandoned disciples in the upper room having their Pentecost moment in Acts 2 went from anxious and hidden to being courageous and visible, led by the spirit of God who gave them a new boldness to preach and teach the message of Jesus at every opportunity. It caused them to be arrested, tried and released with a warning to never speak about Jesus again (Acts 4:18). But that didn't stop them. If anything, the greater the hardship, the more it fuelled their ambition to fulfil the great commission set by their friend and leader, Jesus: to go to the ends of the earth regardless of the consequences.

Stephen, the first Christian martyr, was stoned to death for preaching the message of Jesus. One of those standing by and gloating in this moment was the man Saul, who was on a mission to rid the world of these Jesus followers (Acts 8:1–3). It was official business, authorised by the religious leaders of the day. But God had other plans and met Saul on the Damascus Road, renamed him Paul and caused him to become one of the most influential communicators and church planters in history.

The Church was birthed in difficulties. This is hauntingly summed up in Hebrews 11 where the writer says:

> 'But others were tortured, refusing to turn from God in order to be set free. They placed their hope in a better life after the resurrection. Some were jeered at, and their backs were cut open with whips. Others were chained in prisons. Some died by stoning, some were sawed in half, and others were killed with the sword. Some went about wearing skins of sheep and goats, destitute and oppressed and mistreated.'
>
> Hebrews 11:34–37

The Church has always faced, and will always face, challenges and opposition. Throughout history the Church has encountered and come through the challenges of famine, war, disaster, prejudice, disagreements, reformations, divisions, political fallouts and plagues.

More recently the Church has faced the global coronavirus pandemic, Covid-19, which has affected almost every nation on the planet in one way or another. Churches have been unable to gather in buildings, with some churches in the UK having to close their doors for many months for the first time since the Second World War. At the time of writing, we are still in the middle of a lockdown and all the uncertainty that it brings. And although there has been a creative response from some churches, many have struggled to continue meeting in any meaningful way.

James tells us, 'Consider it pure joy, my brothers and sisters, whenever you face trials of many kinds' (James 1:2 , NIVUK). What an encouraging friend he must have been with his way of lifting your mood on a bad day! The apostle Paul is a little more helpful as he reminds us: 'We are pressed on every side by troubles, but we are not crushed. We are perplexed, but not driven to despair. We are hunted down, but never abandoned by God. We get knocked down, but we are not destroyed' (2 Cor. 4:8–9).

As I write, the Church is right in the middle of a storm, which we will get through. But it is worth noting that although we are in the same storm, we are not all in the same boat. Some are in vast cruise liners and some are hanging onto a piece of driftwood by their fingernails.

Some were prepared and ready, and some were not.

Some hit the storm on empty and are now running on fumes. Others arrived fresh and invigorated by the challenges of something new, but slowly the initial enthusiasm has dissipated as the storm prevails.

The storm you face may look the same as another but each experience is unique.

I have talked with many church leaders who are worried about the future of their church. Here are some of the concerns and struggles they have shared with me:

- Fear about what might happen
- Reliance upon modern technology with an ageing population
- Exhaustion from providing non-stop care and support for their church community while not being able to see people face to face

At the same time, I have been encouraged by stories of churches who have re-invented themselves and found new ways to meet and serve:

- Preaching on street corners
- Drive-in church

- Socially-distanced meetings in parks
- Utilising technology to see more people attending online church than ever before
- Creating pastoral systems of care with regular phone calls
- Food delivery
- Picking up prescriptions
- Setting up or supporting local foodbanks
- Job clubs
- Offering support to those struggling with their mental health
- Finding creative ways to help people recover from financial debt

... Often, just simply loving their neighbour in practical ways.

I'm also encouraged by how Alpha Online is going through the roof, and how tens of thousands of married couples are watching the free online 'Marriage Sessions' from Care for the Family as they navigate the challenge of being in lockdown with their spouse.

The Church is amazing when it faces great discomfort. It is not just a beautiful bride, but a truly creative and resourceful one.

Didn't see it coming

Like most people, I did not see Covid-19 coming. I saw the news of an outbreak in China and thought little more of it. Yes, we would wash our hands more often along to the timing of *Happy Birthday*, but little did we know the disruption that this invisible virus would cause to our health, our finances, our societies or our churches. I had just written the first version of *Simply Church* and within weeks everything was being turned upside down. It felt like I had released a book with the shortest shelf life in history. How could I have not seen it coming?

But this is life. Storms come when we least expect it, whatever the weatherman says. Think classic Michael Fish in October 1987. The question is not will we ever face difficulties in our lives or in our churches, but more how will we cope with them when they happen?

Firstly, never forget, we are not alone. Jesus is with us. You may feel like He is asleep in your boat right now, but I would rather have a sleeping Jesus with me than face the difficulties of life by myself. And besides, I know – along with every child who's been to Sunday school – how the story of Jesus in the boat finishes: 'Peace! Be still' (Mark 4:39, ESVUK).

Secondly, let's make a conscious effort to remember that the Church has faced many, many challenges. As I mentioned earlier in this chapter, we have an incredible track record of hitting some huge hurdles, getting back on our feet and continuing to run the race that has been set before us. We should look back and be encouraged. But don't *keep* looking back. We are not going that way. We want to find a way forward. It is helpful, however, to take a moment to remind ourselves that throughout history the Church has faced unbelievable trouble and torment and yet has outlived empires and dynasties.

As I have often said, we need to go back to the original to create the best copy. The Early Church started in the home. They were unable to build corporately owned church buildings until Emperor Constantine recognised Christianity as a legal religion in 313AD. They relied upon meeting in people's houses, using secret signals to know what time the meeting started. In that challenging time, the Church grew from a handful of people in an upper room in Jerusalem to spreading all over the world with billions of people later referring to themselves as Christians.

Due to Covid-19 our churches may not be able to gather as they used to with one service, or many services across different sites; instead we are simply one Church in many homes. Just like the exponentially growing Church of the first century, who seemed to manage their growth strategy without the help of the worldwide web.

Don't fear the storm

President John F Kennedy famously said in a speech in 1960 that 'In the Chinese language, the word "crisis" is composed of two characters, one representing danger and the other, opportunity.'[42]

This is also true for the Church in every storm we might face. It is both a time of danger and opportunity. We each react differently when faced with difficulty. When faced with a crisis, people will tend to fight or flee. But as churches and followers of Jesus, we are called to be people of faith, not fear. To be people who '[refuse] to turn from God in order to be set free', as we read earlier in Hebrews 11:35. To not choose the easy path, but to face the storm and find a way through.

A crisis can accelerate what is already there. Or as John Maxwell says a 'Crisis does not make character, it reveals character'.[43] We discover our true self in these moments, and we can choose to ignore this or we can realise our need to grow in spiritual maturity – so that we may be better prepared for any subsequent crisis that life will bring along.

If the Church appeared to be experiencing a slow decline before Covid-19, now it looks like the *true* reality has simply been sped up and exposed. People who have left the church were probably going to leave anyway; people who have stayed were already fully committed to the mission of the church. We have discovered that as our reach has got bigger our core has got stronger.

The Church, this vibrant community of believers who have sailed through storm after storm throughout history, will come through again. Probably reshaped, with the loss of some excess baggage such as projects and programmes that had run their course, but potentially more streamlined and focused on its purpose.

Learn in the storm

Difficult seasons, although challenging, are also the times of greatest learning. If we don't fight the change, but instead find ways to respond to the changes that we are facing, we will grow in strength and wisdom. As we have said before: the mission of the Church never changes, but the style must always adapt to the culture it serves. There has been talk about going 'back to normal' once we are post-pandemic; post-crisis. But a healthy church is always moving forwards with the mission, not trying to stay still or desiring to repeat the past to appease existing members. Going back to normal is like digging out your favourite item of clothing from the back of the wardrobe. You know it's worn out, faded and probably not that fashionable anymore, but it has special memories and brings a sense of comfort.

The 'old normal' is like a train that's already left the platform – we can't get back on it. And we will actually be glad to say goodbye to some of it. The 'new normal' is slowly being unboxed and put together, and, I believe, is full of exciting possibilities.

'Our new normal is always feeling a little off balance, like trying to stand in a dinghy on rough seas, and not knowing when the storm will pass.'[44]

Tara Haelle

When you are in a storm, keep going. Hold your nerve and you will come out of it. When a church goes through crisis, hold on. There will be an end to that which we are facing, with something more beautiful to come. Lean into God and follow His blueprint for the Church, which is always in a forward gear. Don't, out of fear, go into reverse and follow the natural desire for safety. Remember that 'God is our refuge and strength, a very present help in trouble' (Psa. 46:1, NIV). Or as Oswald Chambers writes in *My Utmost for His Highest*: 'The river of the Spirit of God overcomes all obstacles. Never focus your eyes on the obstacle or the difficulty. The obstacle will be a matter of total indifference to the river that will flow steadily through you if you will simply remember to stay focused on the Source.'[45]

Dancing in the storm

Author Vivian Greene famously said, 'Life isn't about waiting for the storm to pass, it's about learning to dance in the rain.' So, how do we keep dancing the four principles of *Encounter, Gather, Grow* and *Influence* while we are feeling battered by the storm?

Encounter

This was always meant to be a personal activity, but the modern Church has often turned it into a corporate event. There are dozens of countries where a worship service or a prayer gathering would be illegal, but that has not stopped followers of Jesus from finding new and creative ways to meet and spend time with Him – regardless of the risks that they may be taking. Although a church event can help create a beautiful environment for encounter, it is always the personal responsibility of the individual to connect with God.

However, as is often the case in a consumer-driven, Western world, we can become reliant on the church programme, the prayer room or the Sunday service. But there are so many ways that we can all encounter God. In a storm, everything is disrupted, and this gives us a chance to discover new ways to connect with our creator, whether that be through nature and the outdoors, art and sounds, symbols and routines, caring for others, study of Scripture, or solitude and silence.[46] Whatever it is, we can find new ways to encounter, and enjoy the freedom to choose.

Gather

It's hard to be a community when you can't gather. Not that it's impossible, but it's difficult to intentionally create meaningful community when you don't see one another. It's like when you move to a new area and all your neighbours and friends say they will keep in touch, but they don't as you are no longer a visible reminder to them. The Church is a community, and although technology is helpful to keep in touch with family and friends around the world (and has been essential to those with limited mobility or access to transportation), nothing is the same as spending time with people face to face.

The Church is both spiritual and social. It is the encounter and the gather. You cannot do church in isolation. Gathering is so important and not always fully appreciated until you are unable to meet, whether that be due to persecution, pandemic or accessibility.

But it is worth noting that gathering does not need to be centralised into one big event. As the Early Church met in homes, recent events have helped remind us that we can still be 'One Church, Many Homes'. Even though we might find ourselves scattered across many homes, we are still the Church and we are still one. Gathering is not about attendance or viewing figures.

Gathering is about creating meaningful community, expressed through significant relationships that make us realise that we are loved, needed and known.

Grow

> 'You're not made in a crisis — you're revealed. When you squeeze an orange — you get orange juice. When you squeeze a lemon — you get lemon juice. When a human being gets squeezed — you get what is inside — positive or negative.'
> **Jack Kinder**[47]

When the Christian faces a crisis, the reality of what is going on inside of them leaks out. The same with the local church. When it faces a crisis, the strength of character, community, vision and unity is revealed.

One of the highlights for me of leading my local church through the Covid-19 pandemic of has been watching people in my church dig deep and find a greater depth to their personal faith. They can no longer rely upon the system of events and programmes to stabilise their personal faith or the faith of their children, and so they realise the responsibility lies with them. Strengthening often takes place in a storm. Personal responsibility for discipleship is rediscovered. We were never meant to outsource our growth as Christians.

The Western Church is often guilty of endeavouring to answer spiritual need with a 'one size fits all' variety of events and programmes. Rather than be a guide pointing towards a healthy relationship between God and mankind, it can add layers of complexity that were never intended in the first place. A crisis enables us to see the unnecessary extras for what they are and reboot our spiritual systems back to simply worshipping God.

One of the most successful things for our church during the

pandemic was inviting people to share their stories online by leading morning prayers that we called Daily Freedom. We had all kinds of people taking part: old, young, experienced Christians, new Christians, people who knew how to use technology and people who had no idea how to use their mobile phone to record a video – we saw some sights! But it gave such an insight into people's lives and it broadened the involvement of the church. Everyone had a part to play and we celebrated our diversity in an important moment as we shared the experience of walking through a storm together.

We grow through difficult times. You don't learn much when you have your feet up, sitting on a deck chair in the sun. But, when you are facing uncertainty, your reality leaks out and you have to decide if you going to grow in your faith and lean into God or if you are going to run away in fear. Every crisis is an opportunity to learn something new and gauge how healthy and mature your relationship with Jesus is.

Influence

This is huge for the Church in a crisis. The world often has little time for the Church when everything is working. But when things go wrong, society looks to the Church to see how people of faith are going to respond. After the 9/11 attack in the USA, churches all over the world saw an increase in attendance. When Covid-19 forced people into lockdown, thousands of people in the UK who had never been to church before, especially young people, tried online church.[48] The influence of the local church is often greater than we realise, especially when uncertainty is rife. That influence is always there; it is just not always valued until the local community have need of the local church.

Most churches over the last decade would have some kind of website and social media presence, but the recent pandemic helped us realise that these were not just nice toys to play with. With the internet you can scale your impact like never before. You may be a church of fifty people, but you can reach the world with the message of Jesus through the power of the worldwide web. Post-pandemic, we will go back to our buildings and our Sunday services, but don't let go of the online space that you have discovered. It enables our influence to have a much greater reach. You might never know the impact you are having.

Church is always adapting as it seeks to make a difference. When a crisis requires more, the Church is often one of the first to step up to a new level. I spoke to one church leader who started a foodbank in the middle of the Covid-19 pandemic. They had just built a £5 million pound worship centre, but within weeks of lockdown they had become a lifeline for their local community, serving the needs of those facing poverty and hunger.

That's influence.

Under the bonnet

Every crisis is an opportunity to learn. Find out what works for you and use it effectively. Don't compare yourself to another church – comparison steals all the fun from your calling. It never ends well and takes your eyes off what's really important. Enjoy doing what you do and do it well. Serve the church family, serve your local community as if 'working for the Lord' (Col. 3:23).

Here are some pointers to help you:

• The internet is an amazing gift for the Church. How we communicate, work and play has completely changed in a few short years. The Church may not naturally be an early adopter but we would be foolish to not utilise such a great space to share the gospel to the ends of the earth. Be thankful for the technically minded, the 'geeks' in your Church. If Paul had written the list of ministries in Ephesians 4 today, I wonder whether he would have added the 'office of the geek' to build up the Body of Christ.

- You can do less to achieve more. Don't try to add more to your busy programme. Do less and do it better. Reuse old talks for your online church. Leverage old blogs and content. Don't feel you have to always create something new. Borrow from others. Find new ways to do things by exploring what you already have in your hand.
- Communicate, communicate and then communicate some more. In times of crisis the Church needs to know what is going on. It needs direction, but it also needs to be listened to. Set up ways of communicating and keep listening and talking.
- Use what you've learnt for the future. The Church is going forward, through the storm, adapting for the new normal. What you are learning now may still be valuable once the storm has passed.
- Simplicity can easily get complicated again. We have an inbuilt desire as human beings and organisations to complicate things all of the time. So keep searching for simplicity. And then communicate clearly. Again.

When new challenges come and face the Church, we don't just go with the storm, we assess the situation and work to find a new solution that will get us to the same destination – albeit in a different way to what we had initially planned. The vision doesn't change, but the way we deliver will always need to adapt to the world to which we are speaking.

Remember that Jesus is in the boat *with* you

In a crisis there are challenges and opportunities. Many in the Church saw the invention of the Gutenberg Press in 1450 as unhelpful, but in reality it spawned greater understanding and the ability to share the Christian faith, as millions of Bibles are still sold each year. It was a substantial shift in the way that information was shared, and it impacted the spread of the gospel.

The internet of today, like the motor car of a hundred years ago, or the printing press of 500 years ago, creates a huge opportunity to share the life-changing message of Jesus like never before.

Church is changing. It always has and it always will. Don't put your trust in a church system, a tradition or a way of doing things. Put your trust in Jesus who said, 'I will build my church, and the gates of hell shall not prevail against it' (Matt 16:18, ESVUK).

The Church has a glorious future. It is the *Bride* of Christ. I love the Church and am committed to seeing it succeed throughout the calm and the stormy seasons that it will inevitably face.

> 'and after you have suffered a little while, the God of all grace, who has called you to his eternal glory in Christ, will himself restore, confirm, strengthen and establish you.'
> 1 Peter 5:10, ESVUK

The WHY has a name

Getting married is huge: it's a lifelong commitment, marked by a carefully planned celebration and a very significant transition. Preparing for a wedding can be high-pressured, expensive and stressful. But in her efforts to make the flawless arrangements, a bride can easily end up as 'Bridezilla', spending so much time worrying about herself and making sure her wedding day is perfect that she becomes angry, obsessive, demanding and irrational. A 'Bridezilla' is more focused on her appearance than her future relationship. She is not setting herself up for a healthy marriage – the marriage should always be more important than the wedding day itself.

The Church is the Bride of Christ, but we must never be more obsessed with ourselves and how we look than we are infatuated with the one we are trying to look beautiful for. As the Bride, we need to be prepared, ready and quietly confident in who we are, expressing our love for the one we are primarily there for – Jesus Himself – but we also want to invite as many people as possible to the great wedding feast.

Returning briefly to Sinek's 'golden circle', we need to be clear on our WHAT, our HOW, but most importantly our WHY.

WHAT

All the stuff that has been discussed in this book is important, but it is just stuff.

The mission is still the mission: to go into all the world, preach the gospel and make disciples. The mission will never change.

The way we do church always needs to be adjusted to the world we are trying to connect with, but may we never desire to be so tidy and so relevant that we end up clearing away the very mandate that Jesus gave the Church, just because it looks a bit messy in a modern world and might cause discomfort.

I believe that maybe the Church needs to be less 'polite' – to stop apologising for its very existence and trying to fade into the background of neutrality. We weren't meant to be so concerned about being nice and tidy, saying nothing and becoming an irrelevance because we have nothing to say (or just don't want to offend anyone). I think more gritty determination is required of us. The Church should be open to all, but not so comfortable that it costs us nothing. Christianity is the ultimate challenge, to sacrifice and think of others more than ourselves.

'Simply Church' is purposeful Church – a Church that may tread on some toes and offend those who might otherwise try to keep it in a box. We are not meant to be restrained and limited. We need to be unleashed.

We have a job to do. A mission. A role to play. A purpose, given to us by God Himself – and we need to use the time we have been granted to be effective. We're not here to exist in some kind of waiting room for the real event.

The Church is a vibrant band of adventurers, not a secret club of friends enjoying the comforts of the earth while sitting around in heaven's waiting room, pulling the curtains closed so we don't notice that there is a hurting world out there. We are here to transform the world, in partnership with the Holy Spirit and one another.

To be a Church that will be creative and innovative in sharing the life-changing message of Jesus Christ to our neighbours and the nations.

To be influential, far beyond our natural limits; to regularly see lives transformed through a clear invitation to encounter Jesus.

To be a catalyst to help believers mature in their faith and become fully equipped to lead others.

The Church has been created for this time and for this very purpose.

That is the great commission.

HOW

Remember the ten hallmarks from Acts 2 that we looked at right at the beginning? They are still relevant today. The Early Church has much to teach us. We may live in a high-tech age with time-saving devices, more efficient transport and greater knowledge, but to be authentic, we need to go back to the original.

Let's not get so lost in programmes, events or activities that we forget about the culture we are creating. If our churches are so exhaustively busy with endless activity, nobody will want to come and join in – they will be frazzled just by reading the weekly bulletin, however nice it looks.

Culture is powerful. The way we speak to people, honour people, treat people, says something about who we are. Culture cannot be bought, or even taught – it is caught. It stems from those who lead the church and it will spread like yeast in flour, permeating everything. It is developed over time through what we celebrate, tell stories about, and what we allow to happen. Culture helps make decisions and shapes behaviour. To change it takes a long time, but to become more like the Early Church is worth the effort (and the time will pass anyway).

A more authentic church – Simply Church – is a place where the Bible is taught regularly and unashamedly as the Word of God and the bedrock of our faith, where individuals habitually read the Bible and apply these ancient yet living words to their daily lives. It is known as a vibrant community, where everyone is welcome and there is always room for more – a family that loves eating together and seizing every opportunity to have fun. It is a house of prayer, where we believe anything is possible by the power of the Holy Spirit. It's where we are united and place great value on regularly being together, whether in a large crowd or with only a few. It shows compassion to those in need, always looking for new ways to help others, generous at every opportunity and the first to give. It is known as a place to encounter God, whether through worship at Sunday services or through the deep relationships formed in small groups that meet in homes.

These are the hallmarks of the Early Church.

These are the hallmarks of a detoxed, decluttered, simplified Church.

WHY

The WHY is Jesus.

The answer to 'Why we do church?' is a name, and that name is Jesus. It always has been. The Early Church began because they were friends of Jesus – His gang, His fan club, His family – those who believed in Him so much that they wanted to share this good news story with others. Throughout history it has always been His story that we get to participate in and celebrate with others. You and I are part of the Church today because someone told us the story of Jesus and asked us if we wanted to join the party. The Church is the speaker of truth to all mankind of who Jesus was, is and always will be. It is our core purpose to lead people in the pursuit of Jesus to see lives and communities transformed.

I want to borrow the words of a friend and fellow church leader here:

> I'm not into church (you seen the state of it?) I'm into Jesus, so I like his people. (They're a little weird, but so am I!)
> THE VISION IS JESUS. Not Christianity. Not rules and religion. Not prayer, mission and justice. Not church planting, miracles or mission. Just Jesus.
> If you love Jesus I guess you'll do all that stuff: you'll pray and worship, go to church, preach the gospel, but in doing the stuff, we can so easily forget why. In all the clutter of Christianity we can bury Christ.[41]

In our busyness we can lose Christ. My desire is for us to simplify and declutter our churches. It's not necessarily that we have got it wrong, it's just that we are in danger of damaging our very purpose and soul by burying it under well-intentioned activity, and becoming ineffective in our mission. It's time to defrag and reboot.

It's not about buildings or systems or programmes.

It's not about apps or branding or design.

It's all about Jesus – loving Him, following Him, learning to walk the way He walked.

And when we say it's all about Jesus, what we really mean is, it's all about what Jesus did for us. He gave us all full access to God.

Pointing us to His Father God, His gift of life, His creation, His Son, His sacrifice, His way, His truth, His life.

Ultimately it is His Church.

If you forget everything else, remember this: keep it simple.

Follow the example of Jesus,

who lived a simple life;

spoke simply;

told simple stories;

sat and ate with people, every kind of person;

encouraged His followers to travel light;

and when challenged about what was the greatest commandment, He simply said, 'love the Lord your God with all your heart, all your soul, all your strength and all your mind', and 'Love your neighbour as yourself' (Luke 10:27).

Jesus is WHY the Church does what it does. It is only through Him that we can see families made whole, relationships healed, broken hearts restored and lives and communities truly transformed.

Acknowledgements

Thank you to the team at Waverley Abbey Resources for all their hard work in taking my passion for the local church and helping shape it into a cohesive book that hopefully will serve churches everywhere.

To my wife, Lottie, who has regularly been my personal proof reader and late-night sounding board. Thank you for your unwavering love and support. This book is better because of you and so am I.

To the best children a Dad could ever want – Zak, Levi, Floella and Mimi – thank you for your patience with me as I have hidden myself away to get this book finished.

To my Freedom Church team and family for releasing my time to do this. and for generously allowing me to share some of our story as a vibrant community of Jesus pursuers.

To all my friends who lead churches around the world and have helped shape my thoughts on the Church through so many conversations. I'm still learning, let's not stop talking...

Finally, the greatest thanks and admiration goes to those who serve His Church, in every location across the globe, week in and week out – my thoughts and ideas are just that, but to the ones that put ideas into action, I salute you. You are the true heroes as you live for Jesus and His mission here on earth, leading the local church into everyday life.

Endnotes

[1]Shane Claiborne, Jonathan Wilson-Hartgrove and Enuma Okoro, *Common Prayer: A Liturgy for Ordinary Radicals* (Grand Rapids, MI, USA: Zondervan, 2010)

[2]Richie Norton, *The Power of Starting Something Stupid: How to Crush Fear, Make Dreams Happen, and Live Without Regret* (Salt Lake City, UT, USA: Shadow Mountain, 2013)

[3]You can watch Simon Sinek's TED Talk, 'Start With Why', on Youtube.com and other online video platforms. I also recommend his book, *Start With Why: How Great Leaders Inspire Everyone to Take Action* (New York, NY, USA: Penguin, 2011).

[4]This is a phrase I heard Dave Smith use when speaking at the One Event in 2013 (according to my notes!) and a number of times since.

[5]Raniero Cantalamessa, *Life in the Lordship of Christ: Spiritual Commentary on the Letter to the Romans* (London, UK: Darton, Longman & Todd Ltd, 1992)

[6]Justin Welby was interviewed by Kate Bottley at Greenbelt in 2016. This particular quote is referenced in a Christianity Today magazine article (James Macintryre, 27 August 2016), available online at christianitytoday.com [Accessed December 2019].

[7]John Burke, *No Perfect People Allowed: Creating a Come as You are Culture in the Church* (Grand Rapids, MI, USA: Zondervan, 2005) p97

[8]I heard Andy Stanley say this at the GLS leadership conference in 2015, in Willow Creek, Chicago.

[9]I heard Rick Warren say this in a Q&A session at the HTB Leadership Conference at the Royal Albert Hall. (What can I say, I go to a lot of conferences and take lots of notes. If I can't reference them in a book like this, where else can I use my old notes?)

[10]C.H. Spurgeon, *The Complete Works*, Volume 42: Sermons 2446–2497 (Kindle Edition, Fort Collins, CO, USA: Delmarva Publications, 2012)

[11]I heard Larry Stockstill say this at a church leaders' conference in Peterborough, October 2019.

[12]A selection of psalms that talk about various feasts, festivals and gatherings in the Bible: Psalm 84:10; 122:1; 134, 135:1–2; 149:1; 150.

[13]Simon Benham, *The Peach and the Coconut* (Bracknell, UK: Kerith Media, 2012) p12

[14] Margaret J. Wheatley and Myron Kellner-Rogers, *A Simpler Way* (San Francisco, CA, USA: Berrett Koehler Publishers, 1999) p57

[15]You can do a whole study of the Early Church as a house movement – to get started, have a look at Acts 20:20; Romans 16:5; 1 Corinthians 16:19; Colossians 4:15; Philemon 2; 2 John 10.

[16]OK, so according to Reformation historians, it is unlikely that Martin Luther actually nailed his *95 Theses* to the door of the church (he might have just popped them in the post to his local bishop). Somehow the image of Martin Luther in front of a post box doesn't seem as iconic as hammering a hefty nail through 95 pieces of paper onto a solid wooden door... but either way, these documents had a huge impact across the established Church.

[17]William A. Beckham, *The Second Reformation: Reshaping the Church for the 21st Century* (Houston, TX, USA: Touch Publications, 1995) p25

[18]Ralph Neighbor, *Where do we go from here?* (Houston, TX, USA: Touch Publications, 1990)

[19]Francis Chan, *Letters to the Church* (Colorado Springs, CO, USA: David C. Cook, 2019) p15

[20]Rick Warren, *The Purpose Driven Church* (Grand Rapids, MI, USA: Zondervan, 1995) p130

[21]I love Simon Benham's use of the word 'smorgasbord' describing their church activities in *The Peach and The Coconut* (Bracknell, UK: Kerith Media, 2012)

[22]Paul David Tripp, *Instruments in the Redeemer's Hands* (Phillipsburg, NJ, USA: P&R Publishing, 2002) p116

[23]John Ortberg, *Soul Keeping: Caring for the most important part of you* (Grand Rapids, MI, USA: Zondervan, 2014) p150

[24]Cris Rogers, *Making Disciples: Elevating the conversation around discipleship and spiritual formation* (Uckfield, UK: Essential Christian, 2018)

[25]John Burke, *No Perfect People Allowed: Creating a Come as You Are Culture in the Church* (Grand Rapids, MI, USA: Zondervan, 2007)

[26]I love the image this phrase creates, which is also the title of Eugene Peterson's book, *A Long Walk of Obedience in the Same Direction* – which is more than just a title but a lifestyle that Eugene, as an author and a church pastor, fully embraced.

[27]Scott Wilson, *G Factor: Using Vision, Values, Goals and Strategy to Grow a Church* (Roskilde, Denmark: ApoNet, 2011)

[28]Rich Hubbard, *The Promise of the Holy Spirit is for You* (Powerpoint Publications, 1984)

[29]Both quotes taken from Alan Scott, *Scattered Servants: Unleashing the Church to bring life to the city* (Colorado Springs, CO, USA: David C. Cook, 2018)

[30]Rick Warren, *The Purpose Driven Church* (Grand Rapids, MI, USA: Zondervan, 1996)

[31]The famous 'Anyway' poem has often been attributed to Mother Teresa, but it is actually based on the writings of 19-year-old Harvard student Kent Keith, published by Harvard Student Agencies in 1968. Kent did not realise that his work had been plagiarised by the great Mother Teresa until after she had died and he heard 'her' poem read aloud at his Rotary Club almost 30 years after he had first published it.

[32]If you're interested you can read the full Cinnamon Network Faith Action Audit report here: cinnamonnetwork.co.uk/cinnamon-faith-action-audit [Accessed December 2019]

[33]Gavin and Anne Calver, *Unleashed: The Acts Church Today* (London, UK: IVP, 2020)

[34]Whenever anything's referred to as an African proverb, it probably means it is not an African proverb... just an ancient saying with no way of proving where it first came from. That seems to apply here.

[35]For more information, head to eauk.org/what-we-do/networks/one-people-commission [Accessed December 2019]

[36]I recommend Craig Groeschel's Leadership Podcast, widely available.

[37]John Maxwell, *The 21 Irrefutable Laws of Leadership* (Nashville, TN, USA: Thomas Nelson, 2007) p267

[38]This line comes from a foreword written by the great Arthur Wallis in Philip Greenslade's original edition of *Leadership* (London, UK: Marshall Morgan & Scott, 1984)

[39]Patrick Lencioni, *The Five Dysfunctions of a Team: A Leadership Fable* (Hoboken, NJ, USA: John Wiley and Sons, 2002)

[40]You can read Tim Keller's full article at seniorpastorcentral.com – search for 'Leadership and Church Size Dynamics: How Strategy Changes with Growth'. [Accessed December 2019]

[41]Pete Greig (@PeteGreig) tweeted this on 21 May, 2019, and has given permission to reprint it here. He elaborates on this further in *Dirty Glory* (London: Hodder & Stoughton, 2016) pp56–57

[42]President Kennedy at Valley Forge Country Club, Valley Forge, Pennsylvania, 29 October 1960

[43]John Maxwell, *The 21 Indispensable Qualities of a Leader* (Nashville, TN, USA: Thomas Nelson, 1999) p3

[44]Tara Haelle, 'Your Surge Capacity is Depleted – It's Why You Feel Awful', Elemental, https://elemental.medium.com/your-surge-capacity-is-depleted-it-s-why-you-feel-awful-de285d542f4c (Accessed January 2021)

[45]Oswald Chambers, My Utmost for his Highest 'March 19', (Discovery Books, 1992)

[46]Gary Thomas, Sacred Pathways: Discover Your Souls Path to God (1996)

[47]Jack Kinder Jr & Jayne Kinder Clement, *Unforgettable: Maxims Revisited & Memories Restored* (The Gray Group, 1998)

[48]'British public turn to prayer as one in four tune in to online services', www.theguardian.com/world/2020/may/03 (Accessed January 2021)

Resources you may find helpful

Encounter

• Pete Greig, *How to Pray: A Simple Guide for Normal People* (London: Hodder & Stoughton, 2019)

• Mike Pilavachi and Andy Croft, *Everyday Supernatural: Living a Spirit-Led Life Without Being Weird* (David C. Cook, 2016)

• Matt Redman, *Face Down* (Regal Books, 2004) and *The Unquenchable Worshipper: Coming Back to the Heart of Worship* (Bethany House Publishers, 2001). These may be some of Matt's older books, but they get right to the point on our call to worship God both inside and outside church.

• Mark Sayers, *Reappearing Church* (Moody Press, 2019)

• Andy Stanley, *Deep & Wide: Creating Churches Unchurched People Love to Attend* (Zondervan, 2016)

• The Prayer Course by 24-7 Prayer (prayercourse.org) – I particularly recommend its 'Prayer Toolshed' with 30 tools to help you pray more effectively.

• Worship U by Bethel Music (worshipu.com), training worship leaders and musicians via their online worship school.

• Worship Central (worshipcentral.org) is an academy for worship training, an online collective of musicians, and an annual event led by worship legend Tim Hughes.

Gather

• Alpha (alpha.org) – the Alpha course is a friendly, easy access 12-week course for anyone looking to discover more of the Christian faith. I think every church should run one!

• Francis Chan, *Letters to the Church* (Gospel Light, 2019)

• Messy Church (messychurch.org.uk) suggests loads of fresh ideas about how you gather 'non-church' communities together.

• Open Network (open.life.church) provides free resources for the Church, including teaching series, children's programmes, youth downloadables and even church building designs you can have for free!

• There are some brilliant small group courses available online (store.pastors. com). Rick Warren is a huge fan of small groups – at Saddleback Community Church, which he leads, they frequently have more people attending their small groups than their weekend services. He has collected dozens of incredible resources that will help bring life to any small group programme.

• The Kitchen Table Project by Care for the Family has been set up to help families nurture faith around the table in the home. Search for 'Kitchen Table Project' at careforthefamily.org.uk

• If you are struggling to find children's activities for your Sunday or mid-week groups, I highly recommend Energize by Urban Saints (energize.uk.net). Access requires a small monthly payment, but this is an amazing resource with access to hundreds of materials that can be edited to suit the time you have available and the age group of your kids.

Grow

• YouVersion (YouVersion.com) is a free Bible tool for every version of the Bible you can imagine, plus a variety of excellent reading programmes. You can also link with others in your church and interact online with your daily devotional experiences.

• Cris Rogers, *Making Disciples*, is a book, app and course that will help you develop your understanding of discipleship in your church. It will challenge the individual and change the community (wearemakingdisciples.com).

• Peter Scazzaro, *Emotionally Healthy Spirituality* (Zondervan, updated 2017) is another one of those books that's become a course – and an excellent one at that. If you have a church full of mature Christians who feel like they have got a bit stuck, then this is the course for you (emotionallyhealthy.org).

• Waverley Abbey Resources offers a wide range of Bible reading resources, including the classic *Every Day with Jesus*. It's been around a while but is still one of the most popular daily devotionals (waverleyabbeyresources.org/edwj). We hand them out in our New Believer's Packs in our church and encourage people to make use of them. Lots of people still like a paper book!

• Lectio 365 (available from your app store) is a new devotional app developed by Waverley Abbey Resources in partnership with 24-7 Prayer. If you want to mix up your prayer life and your Bible reading, then this is a great resource with contributions from Pete Greig and his team, to get you connecting with God daily.

• 24-7 Prayer have also developed the Inner Room app, which encourages you to pray regularly and pause before rushing on with your day.

• Bible in One Year (bibleinoneyear.org) is another great online daily devotional that goes through the whole Bible over the course of a year. You can start whenever you want and join in straightaway.

• Prayer Mate is another app that helps you link with other members of your church (for a small fee) and pray together with fully editable prayer lists. If technology is your thing, then this works well.

Influence

• John Burke, *No Perfect People Allowed* (Zondervan, 2007)
• Alan Scott, *Scattered Servants: Unleashing the Church to Bring Life to the City* (David C. Cook, 2018)

There are so many good church-based projects out there to help your church transform your local community, but here are some favourites:

• Christians Against Poverty (CAP) (capuk.org) – The work of CAP has made such a difference to so many people in our church – those who serve as volunteers, and those who have received help in going debt free.

- Food banks by The Trussell Trust (trusselltrust.org) – We helped set up the local food bank in partnership with all the other churches in our town. The support from The Trussell Trust was excellent as we partnered nationally to make a local difference.

- Transforming Lives for Good (TLG) (tlg.org.uk) – Having won the Sunday Times award in 2019 for Best Not for Profit to Work For and Best Leader for their CEO Tim Morfin, this is an excellent and high quality organisation that helps churches serve local schools, from early intervention to full-on school provision for pupils at risk of exclusion. TLG exists to help churches bring hope and a future to struggling children.

- The Cinnamon Network (cinnamonnetwork.co.uk) – The 'check a trade' of Christian charities. Cinnamon provide huge amounts of projects, resources and grant funds to get churches up and running in serving their community. They are keen to do anything they can to strengthen the muscles of the local church.

Under the Bonnet

- Mark Driscoll and Gerry Breshears, *Vintage Church: Timeless Truths and Timely Methods* (Crossway Books, 2009).

- Rick Warren, *The Purpose Driven Church* (Zondervan, 1996). This is one of the first books I read when I moved into church leadership, and it's still a great practical book to help organise your church in outreach, growth and discipleship.

- If you want to know anything about money and the UK Church, there's loads of helpful stuff available from Stewardship (stewardship.org). From giving, tithing, mortgages for buildings, saving, church payroll or just a better understanding of how we are called to steward what we have been given, this is highly recommended.

- Dave Ramsey is an American speaker on matters of finance. He is a Christian version of the UK's Martin Lewis, who offers financial advice and saving tips, but also specialises in financial health for churches. His website is well worth a look (daveramsey.com/churchwide).

• Robert Morris, *The Blessed Church* (Waterbrook Press, 2014). One of the most helpful resources on financial giving that I have come across.

• Craig Groeschel Leadership Podcast (life.church/leadershippodcast) – If you want to grow in your church leadership, then this is the podcast for you. There are so many options out there, but Craig Groeschel makes learning about leadership accessible to all.

• Global Leadership Network (globalleadership.org) – Having had the pleasure of attending the Annual Event that takes place in Chicago each summer, I can highly recommend the incredible standard of leadership content that is produced each year. Don't worry if you can't make it to the US, they also do a UK tour every autumn, which is worth going along to with other members of your church team.

• Anything by John Maxwell, literally. John is the guru of leadership. The first book on leadership that I was ever given was *Developing the Leaders Around You*. But he has written dozens of books, and also has a podcast and website... you know the drill.

• At Freedom Church we love Church Suite (churchsuite.com) – The ultimate back-office tool that runs the church so you don't need to! This comes from a UK church that are keen to serve churches everywhere to become more effective. It is a smartphone app that can run your giving and Gift Aid, your small groups, your Sunday programme, your rotas, your database and communications – it just works.

Every day with Jesus

Join in with thousands of readers around the world in encountering Jesus every day.

Find revelation and encouragement with readings, thoughts, prayers and actions to take. Be enriched in your faith and see its impact in all areas of life.

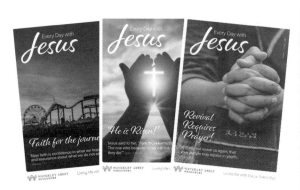

Printed subscription
FREE in the UK (costs apply internationally)

Email subscription
FREE

Ebook
Costs apply

Every Day with Jesus on YouVersion App
FREE

PDF Download
FREE

Audio Version
FREE

To find out more and access, visit
waverleyabbeyresources.org/edwj

WAVERLEY ABBEY
RESOURCES

WAVERLEY ABBEY TRUST

COLLEGE
RESOURCES
HOUSE

waverleyabbeycollege.ac.uk   waverleyabbeyresources.org   waverleyabbeyhouse.org

Waverley Abbey Trust

We are a charity serving Christians around the world with practical resources and teaching. We support you to grow in your Christian faith, understand the times in which we live, and serve God in every sphere of life.

Bible Engagement
Waverley Abbey Trust provides many ways to encounter God in the Bible, especially through *Every Day with Jesus*, our other daily Bible reading notes, our publications and our courses.

Prayer
We are passionate about rooted in prayer. We help people to go deeper in prayer through resources like the Lectio 365 App we created with 24-7 Prayer, and we have a prayer community onsite.

Mental Wellbeing
Through our Higher Education programmes at Waverley Abbey College, we train Christians to become professional counsellors. Additionally, we produce resources in the areas of mental and emotional health, specifically our *Insight* range.

Leadership
We support leaders in articulating and realising their vision, influencing the context in which they lead and empowering those they lead through our training, resources and conferencing centre.

Spiritual Formation
Our Higher Education training, short courses and resources help people to deliberately open up their lives for a deeper connectedness with God, and in doing so become more of who He made them to be.

waverleyabbey.org